Big Chinese Workbook for Little Hands
小手写中文

Written by Yang Yang

Consulting Editors: Claire Wang, Qin Chen, Han Xu, Yi Chen, Ke Peng

这是＿＿＿＿＿＿的书。

This book belongs to:

_____

Copyright © 2017 by Yang Yang.

All rights reserved. No part of this publication may be reproduced, stored in a retrieval system or transmitted in any form without written permission from the publisher.

ISBN: 978-1974065929

www.bigchineseworkbook.com

Dear Parents,

Big Chinese Workbook for Little Hands is a series of Chinese workbooks specifically designed for children living in English speaking countries and/or regions. Since its first publication in April of 2016, this workbook has soon become a bestseller in children's Chinese Language Books across the United States.

Upon completion of Level 2, your child should be able to:

- Identify and write 22 commonly used radicals in addition to the ones learned in Level 1.
- Adapt to the correct stroke order when writing Chinese characters.
- Understand and use 14 pairs of antonyms.
- Write 8 types of simple sentences and arrange word orders.
- Talk briefly about the world, people, language and culture.
- Read up to 300 new characters and write about 120 of them (including 16 more sight words).

Total vocabulary for Level K+ Level 1+Level2
Reading: 850   Writing: 285

A sound recording is available for most pages in this book. Scan the QR code on each page to listen to it or scan the one on the front cover to access all soundtracks. For optimized learning, please use *Tracing and Writing Chinese Characters, Level 2* along with this book. You may also get one of our Tian Zi Ge notebooks for more writing practice.

养成这样的习惯，学习效果会更好：

1. 每次做练习之前，都大声朗读上一次做过的部分，再默写一次写过的字。
2. 学写一个生字的时候，（在老师或家长的指导下）边写边说出笔画的名称。比如写"口"的时候，就边写边说竖、横折、横。
3. 每个生字描写两遍、抄写一遍以后，就遮住写过的字，试着自己默写（最后两格）。
4. 鼓励孩子用每个生字组词或造句。

祝您的孩子中文进步！

楷书 Regular Script

Starting from Level 2, Regular Script (楷书, or 楷体) is used throughout the book. After two years training in writing strokes, radicals, and characters in Boldface (黑体), students now have a better understanding of the Chinese writing system and have improved their handwriting skills. Hence the most commonly used font, Regular Script, is adopted and recommended for use in handwriting from now on.

Evolution of Chinese Characters

甲骨文 Oracle Bone Script	♛	☽	雨
金文 Bronze Script	♛	☽	雨
篆书 Seal Script	山	☾	雨
隶书 Clerical Script	山	月	雨
行书 Running Script	山	月	雨
草书 Cursive Script	山	月	雨
楷书 Regular Script	山	月	雨
黑体 Boldface	山	月	雨

Write in Regular Script with a Chinese writing brush. If you don't have one, simply use your finger tip and some watercolor paint. Follow the directions when writing. Start from the •, press and turn at the ▾, and release at the ↓.

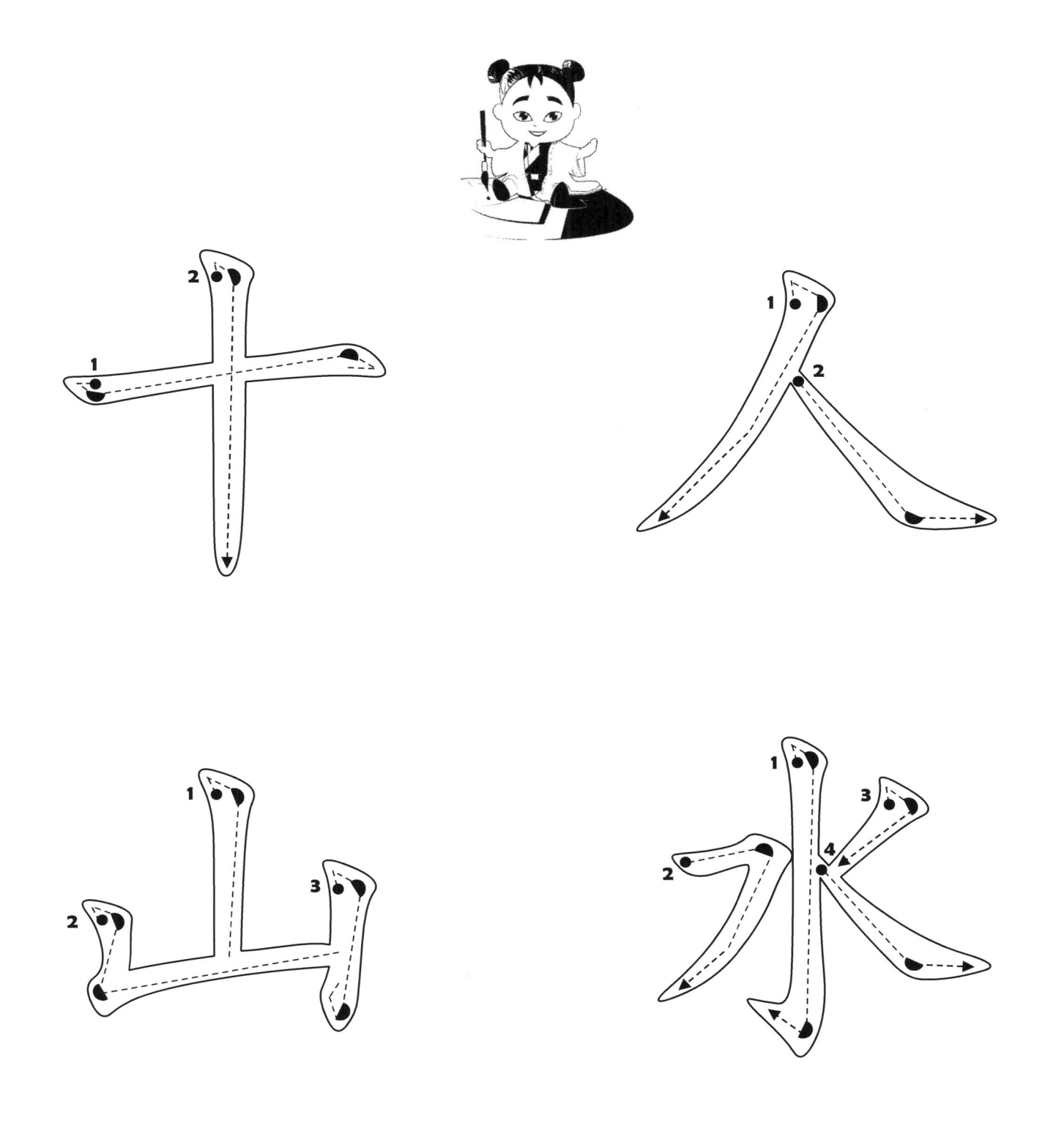

When writing in Regular Script with a pencil, we simplify the steps and only do the pressing and the releasing. Trace the following words in Regular Script with a pencil. Press on the • and release at the ↓.

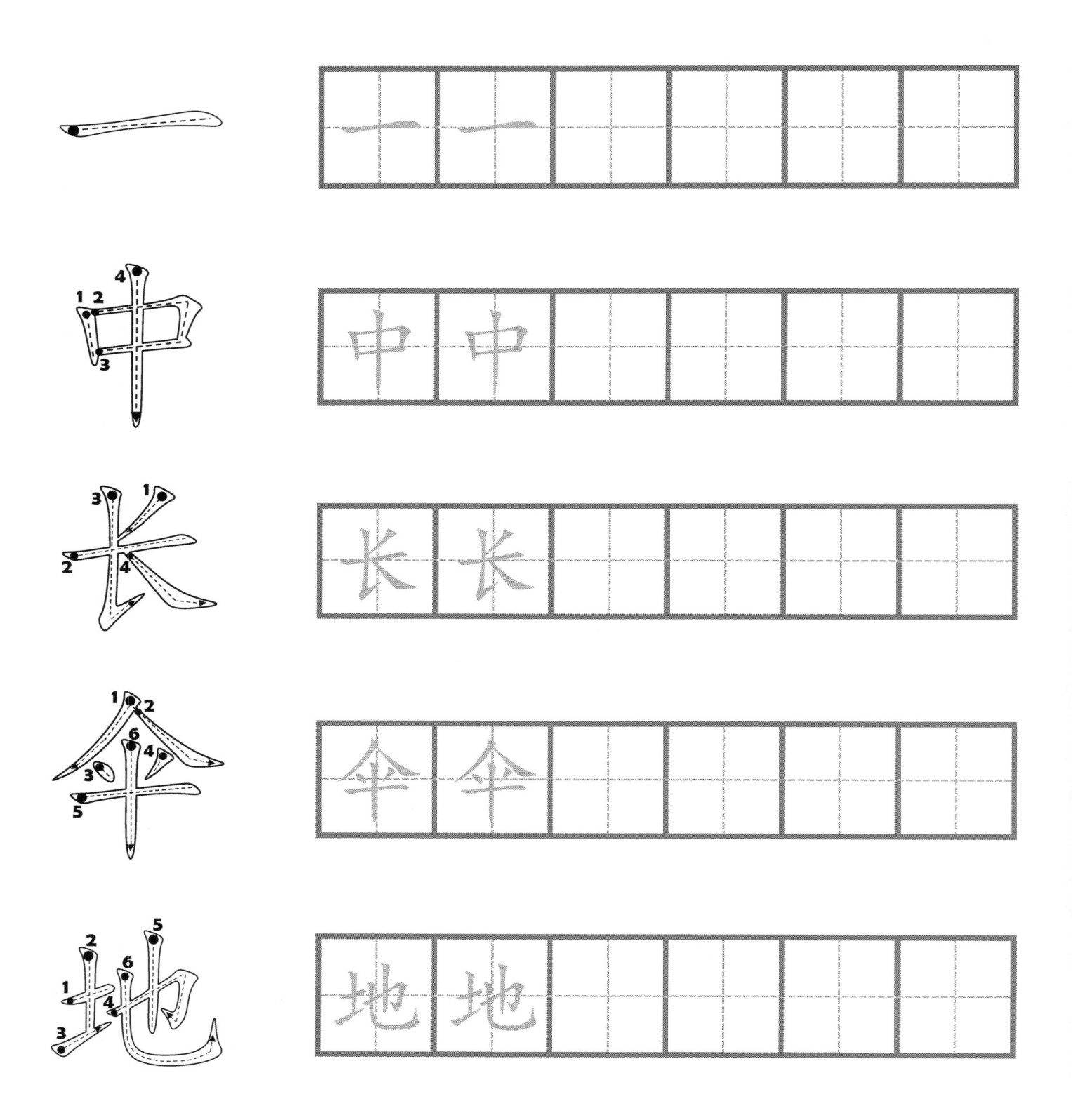

Contents

Semantic Radicals ---------------------------------- 6
部首练习

Opposites ---------------------------------- 68
反义词

Sight Words ---------------------------------- 98
最常用字

Sentence Structure ---------------------------------- 128
句型结构

People and Culture ---------------------------------- 146
人文

Answers are downloadable at
www.BigChineseWorkbook.com

部首练习

Semantic Radicals

部首练习
Semantic Radicals

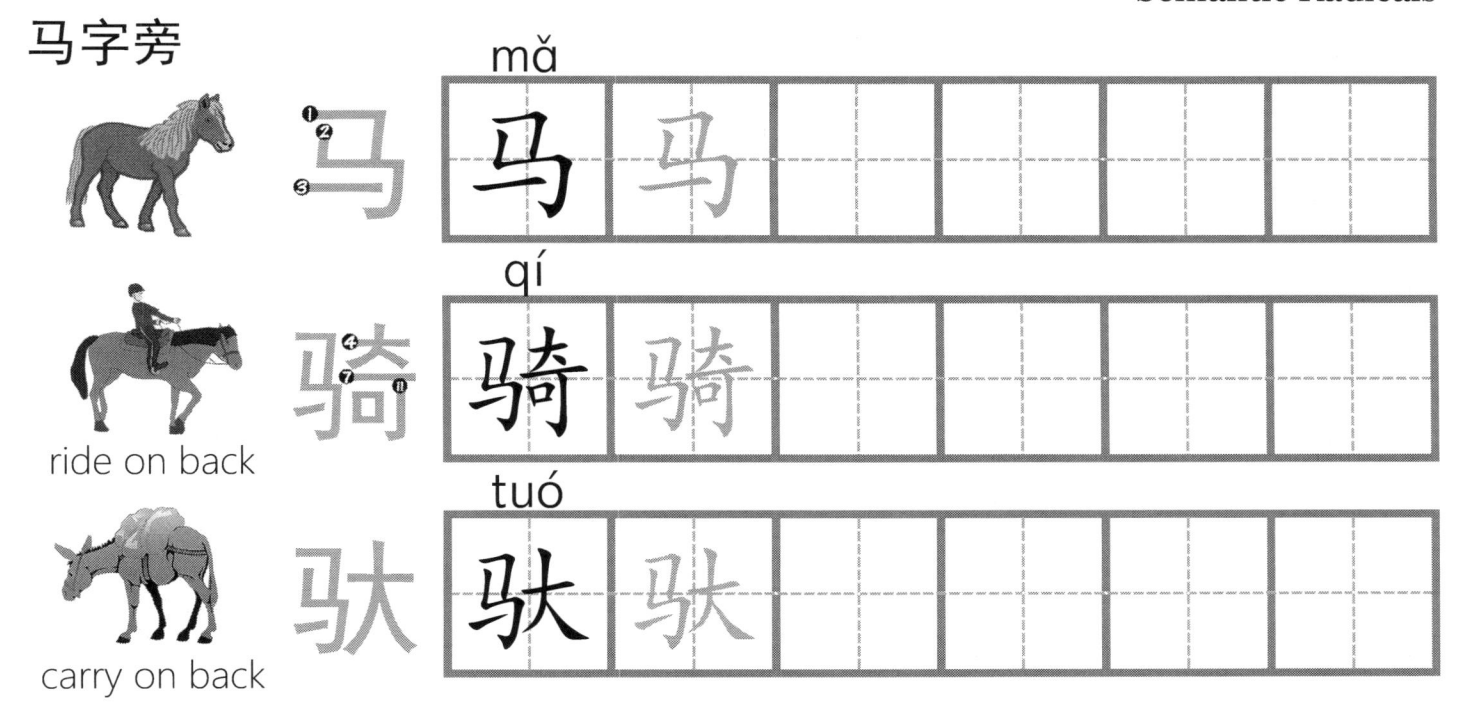

马字旁

mǎ
马

ride on back
qí
骑

carry on back
tuó
驮

Find and trace 马 in these characters.

河马
hippo

bān
斑马
zebra

lú
毛驴
donkey

luò tuó
骆驼
camel

qí
骑车

jiāo ào
骄傲
proud, arrogant

piàn
骗子
cheater

7

Make words with 马 and fill in the blanks.

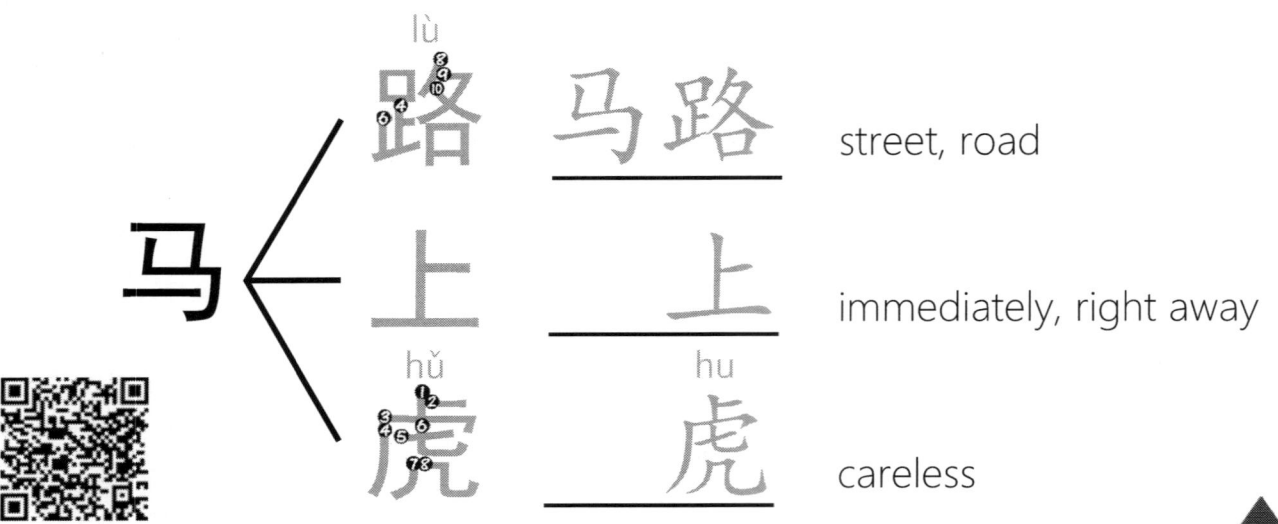

马 ←
- 路 (lù) 马路 ____ street, road
- 上 上 ____ immediately, right away
- 虎 (hǔ) 虎 (hu) ____ careless

1. 我家门口有一条____马路____。
2. 快回家！____要下雨了。 (kuài / it's going to rain)
3. 弟弟写字有点儿____。

Fill in the correct word for each sentence.

1. 毛驴___大米。（骑 驮） 
2. 哥哥___自行车。（骑 驮）
3. 马和羊___爱吃青草。（也 都） 
4. 毛驴____骆驼高。（比 没有）

8

部首练习
Semantic Radicals

金字旁　金 ➡ 钅

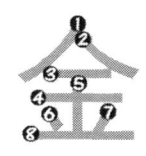

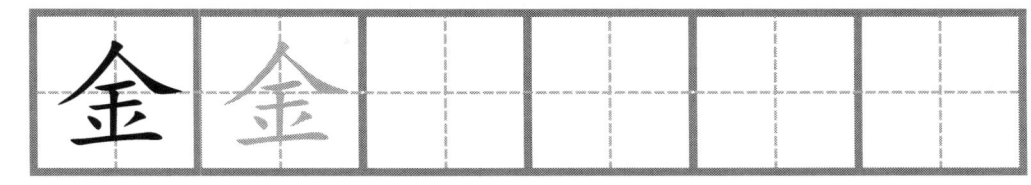

gold

metal radical

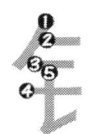

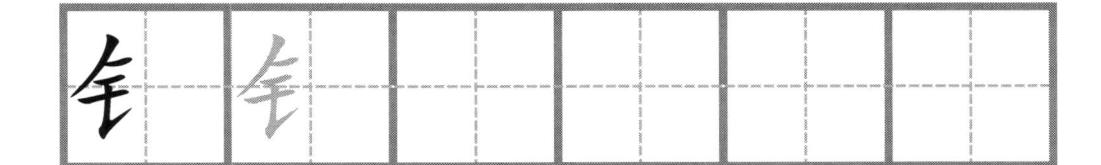

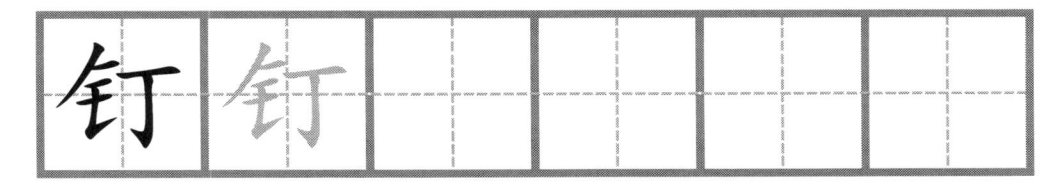

钉子 nail

Find and trace 钅 in these characters.

qiān bǐ
铅笔
pencil

gāng
钢笔
pen

yào shi
钥匙
key

qián
钱
money

diào
钓鱼
fishing

zhēn
打针
give an injection

líng
门铃
doorbell

zhōng
钟
clock

9

Fill in the blanks with characters in the box.

铅　　钱　　钓　　钥

1. 粉笔短，____笔长。

2. 西瓜四块____一个。

3. 我会用____匙开门。

4. 小猫____上来一条大鱼。

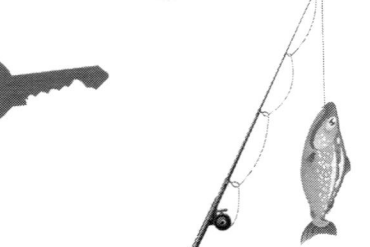

Substitute the radical to make characters with 钅 and then use it in a word.

~~明~~ + 钅 ➡ <u>钥</u> （钥匙）

~~灯~~ + 钅 ➡ ＿＿ （　　）

~~的~~ + 钅 ➡ ＿＿ （　　）

~~什~~ + 钅 ➡ ＿＿ （　　）

~~冷~~ + 钅 ➡ ＿＿ （　　）

部首练习
Semantic Radicals

All kinds of 镜 (jìng, lens). Fill in the blanks with 镜.

1. 姐姐戴眼____看书。(dài / glasses)

2. 弟弟用放大____看毛毛虫。(magnifier)

3. 爸爸用望远____看星星。(wàngyuǎn / telescope)

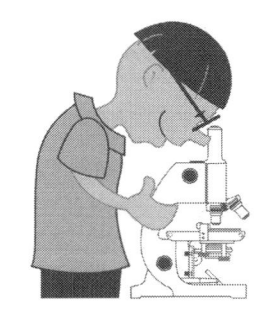

4. 我用显微____看树叶。(xiǎn wēi / microscope)

5. 妈妈照____子梳头。(zhào / shū / look in the mirror (when) combing hair)

6. 我们都戴太阳眼____去海边。(sunglasses)

11

Read the story and number the pictures in the correct order.

小猫钓鱼

猫妈妈和小猫去钓鱼。

1. 蜻蜓飞来了，小猫去捉蜻蜓。
   (qīngtíng) (zhuō / capture)

2. 蝴蝶飞来了，小猫去捉蝴蝶。
   (hú dié)

3. 猫妈妈钓了很多鱼，小猫一条鱼也没钓到。
   (hěn / many) (did not catch)

猫妈妈说："钓鱼要一心一意，不要三心二意。"
(yì / should be whole-hearted) (half-hearted)

4. 一会儿，蜻蜓飞来了，小猫没看它。
   ((after) a while)

5. 蝴蝶飞来了，小猫也没看它。

6. 小猫钓上来一条大鱼，很开心。

12

刀字底／立刀旁　　刀 ➡ 刂　　　　　　　　　　　　　部首练习
　　　　　　　　　　　　　　　　　　　　　　　　　Semantic Radicals

dāo
刀

knife radical
刂

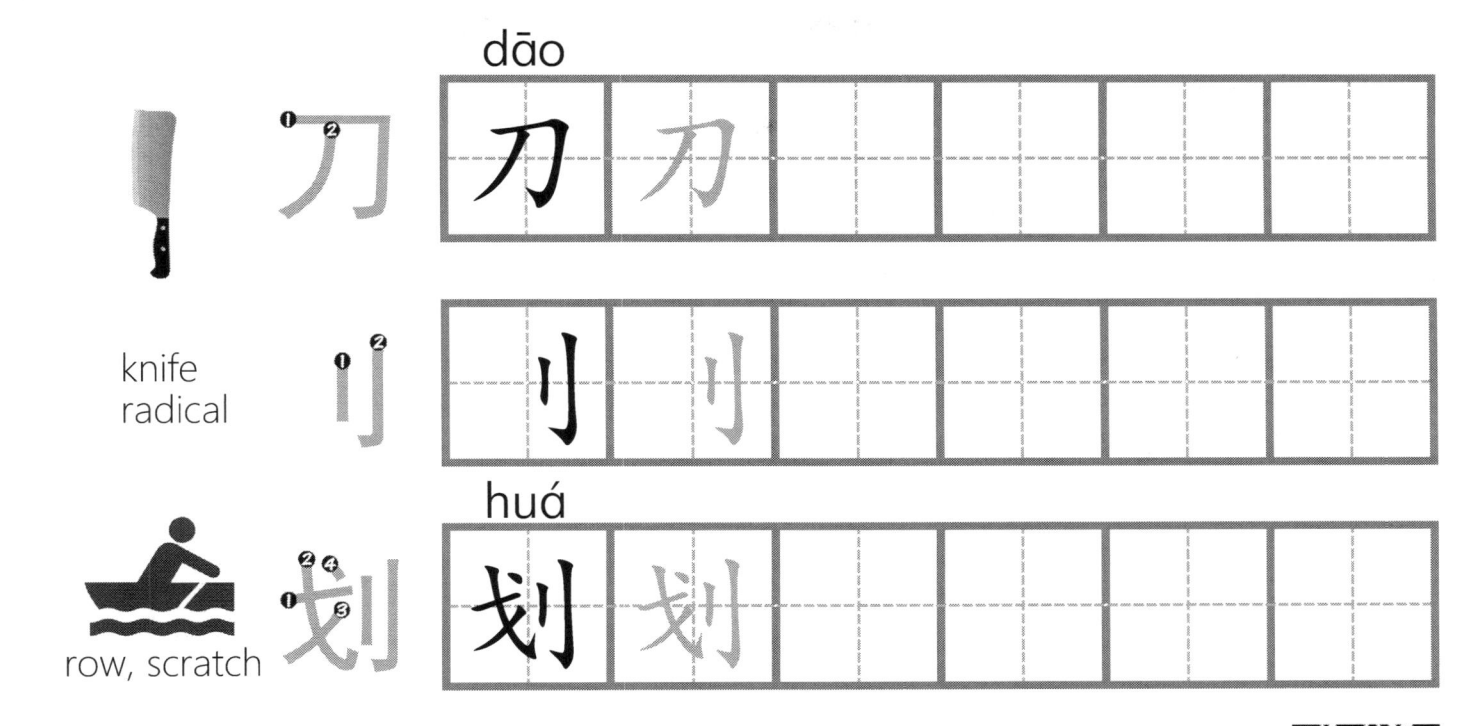

huá
划
row, scratch

Find and trace 刀／刂 in these characters.

jiǎn
剪刀
scissors

qiē
切面包
cut

gē
割草
mow

shuā
刷牙

chuán
划船
row a boat

bié
别针
pin

别人
other people

别哭
don't cry

13

Find and trace 刀/刂 in these characters. Then fill in the blanks with characters in the box.

前天　　　一分钟　　　一刻钟
　　　　　 a　minute　　a quarter (of an hour)

cái
刚才　　　　来到　　　　别人
just now　　arrive

fēn	kè	gāng		bié
前 分	刻	刚	到	别

1. 从我家走路____学校要十五分钟。

2. 十五____钟等于一____钟。
　　　　　　 děng yú
　　　　　　 equal

3. 昨天是星期五，____天是星期四。
   zuó
   yesterday

4. ____才有人按门铃。
　　　　　 àn
　　　　　 press (ring)

5. 这不是我的，是____人的。

6. 现在是两点一____。　　02:15

14

王字旁（斜玉旁） 玉 ➡ 王

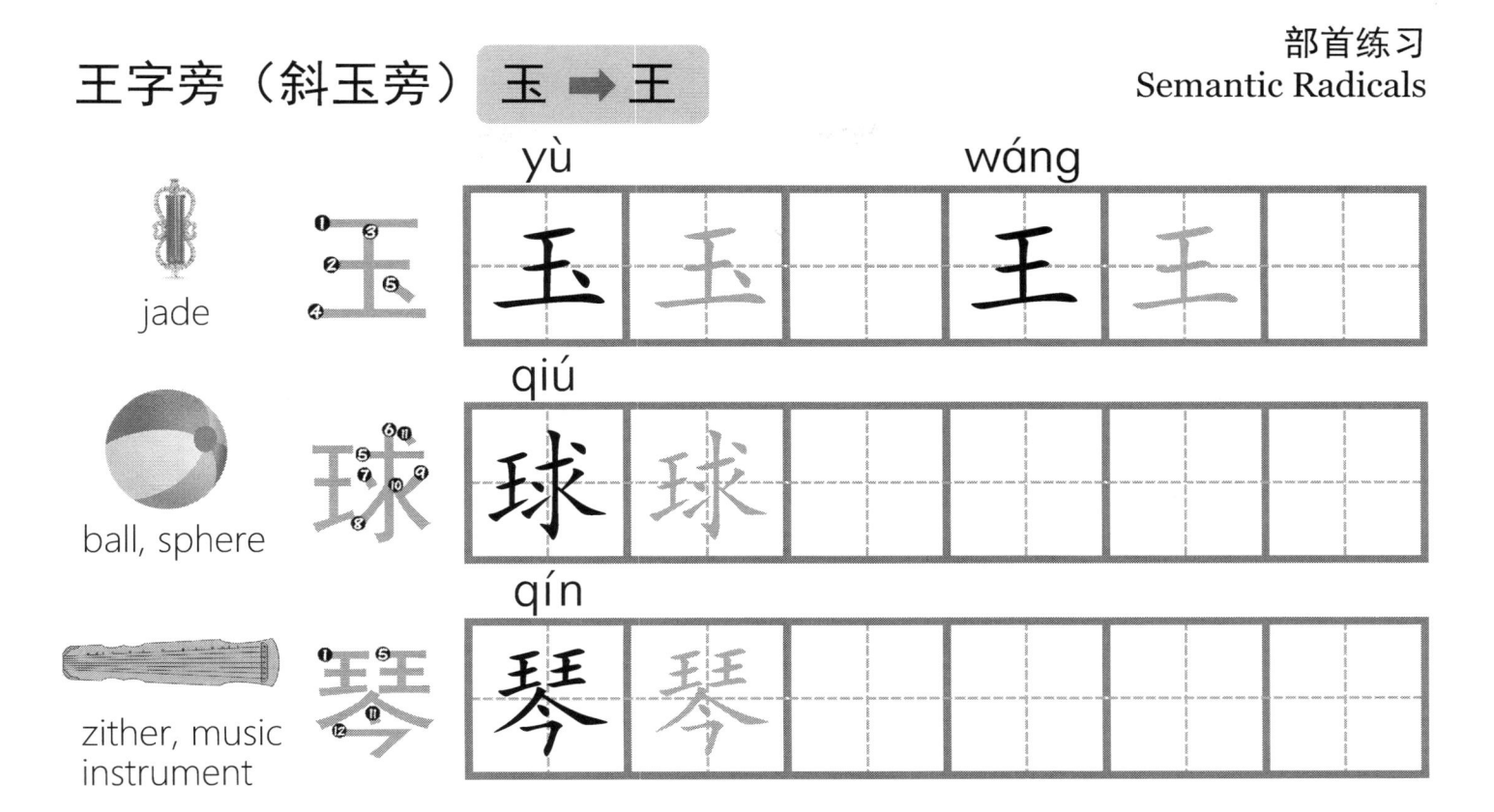

部首练习
Semantic Radicals

yù　　　　　　　wáng
玉　玉　　　王　王

jade

qiú
球　球

ball, sphere

qín
琴　琴

zither, music instrument

Find and trace 王 in these characters.

钢**琴**

wán　jù
玩具
toy

bān
斑马

bō　li
玻璃杯
glass

huán
耳**环**
earring

地**球**

bān
上**班**
go to work

15

Make words with 球. Use the character box for hint.

足 拍 地 星 月 衣

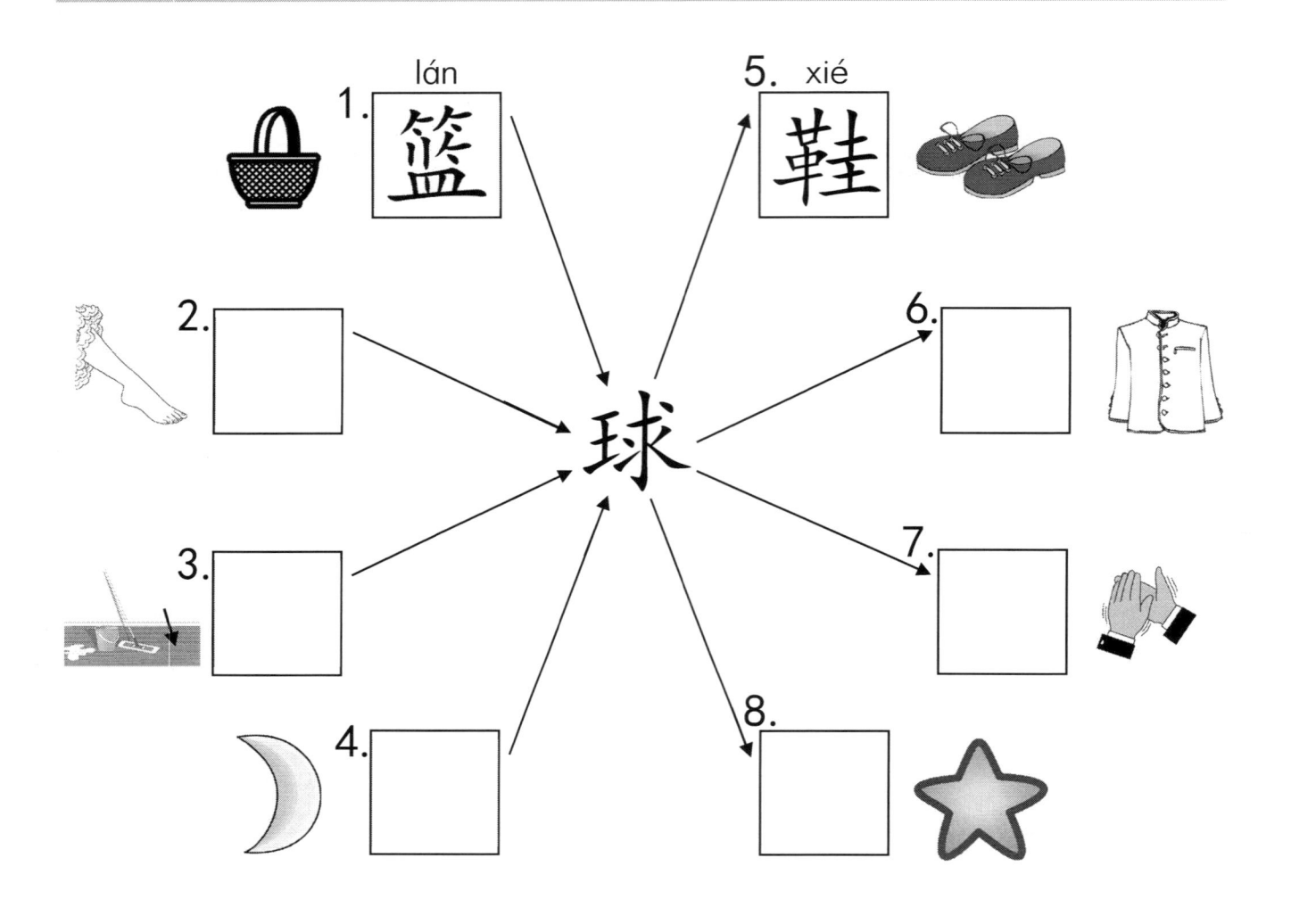

1. lán 篮
5. xié 鞋

球

1. 篮____
2. ____
3. ____
4. ____
5. ____鞋
6. ____
7. ____
8. ____

竹字头 竹 ➡ 竹

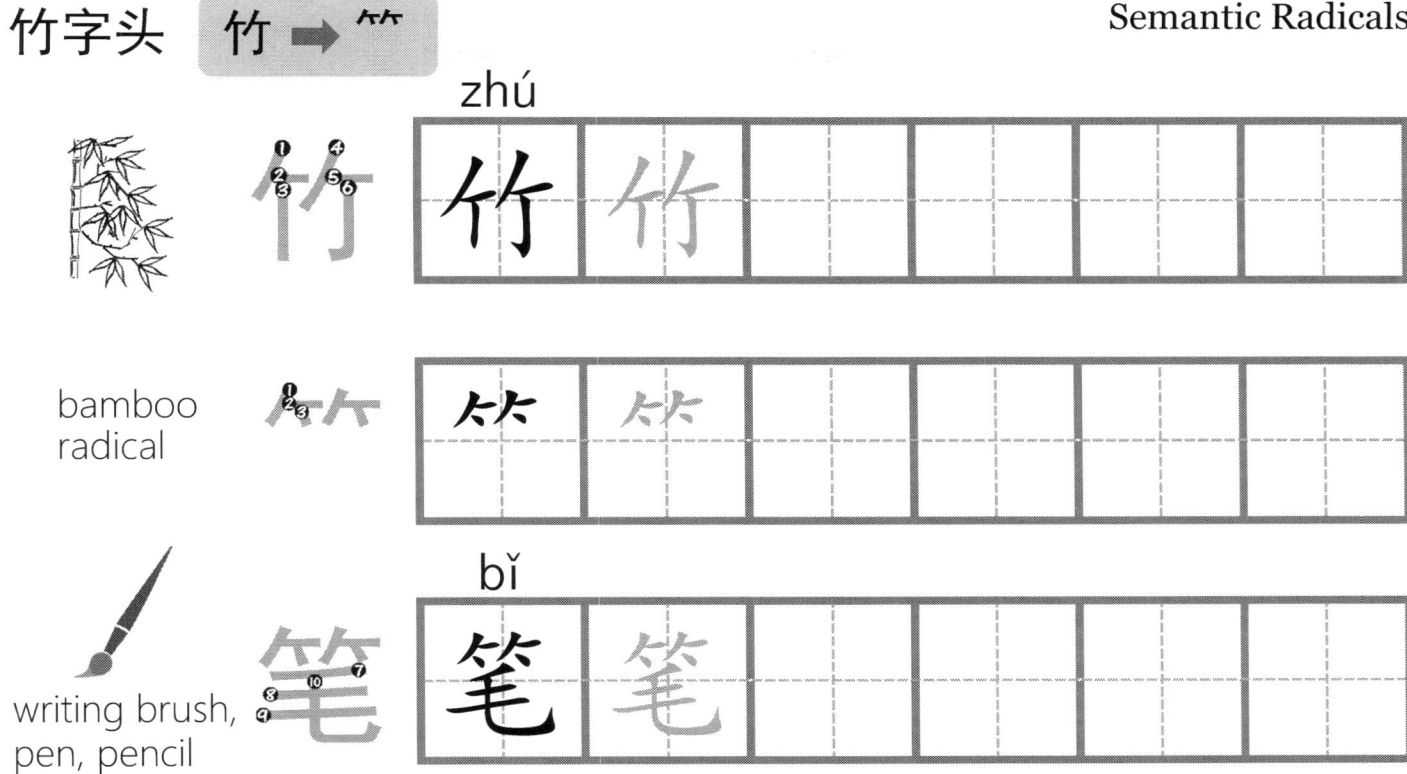

部首练习
Semantic Radicals

zhú
竹

bamboo radical
竹

bǐ
笔

writing brush, pen, pencil

Find and trace 竹/⺮ in these characters.

lán
篮子
basket

篮球
basketball

kuài
筷子
chopstick

xiāng
冰**箱**
(ice box) fridge

zhēng
风**筝**
kite

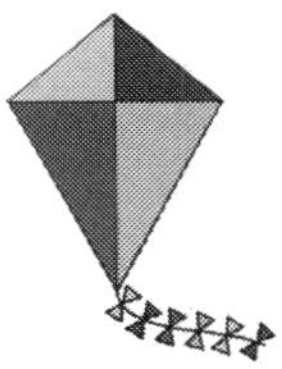

gōng jiàn
弓**箭**
bow and arrow

火**箭**
rocket

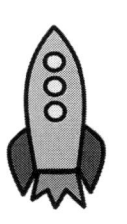

gān
钓鱼**竿**
fishing rod

17

All kinds of 笔. Complete the words with 笔.

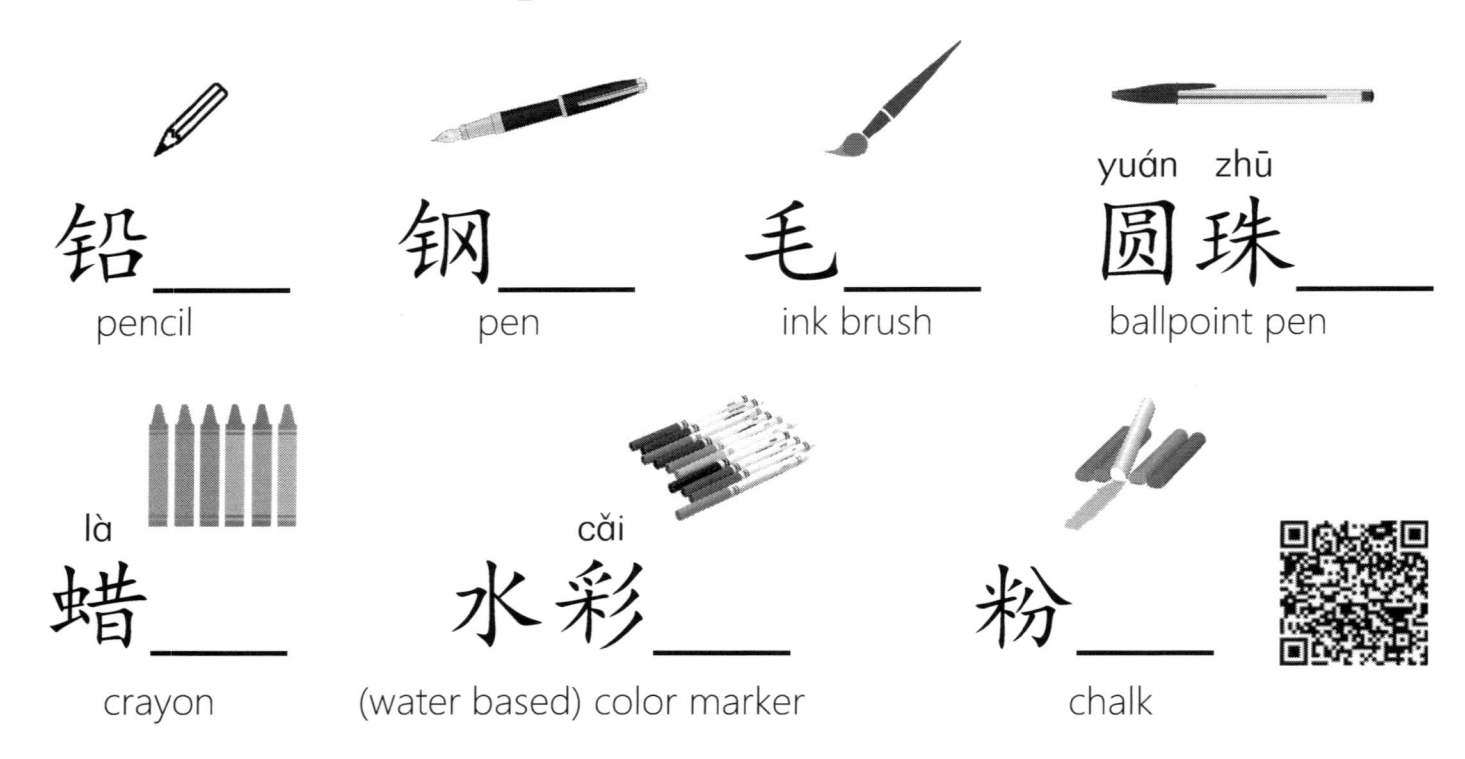

铅___ 钢___ 毛___ 圆珠___
pencil　　pen　　ink brush　　ballpoint pen

là
蜡___　　水彩___　　粉___
crayon　　(water based) color marker　　chalk

Fill in the blanks with characters in the box.

竹　筷　箱　筝　箭

1. 春天我放风___，夏天我游泳。

2. 火___上了天。

3. 中国人吃饭用___子。

4. 熊猫爱吃___子。

5. 冰___里有很多好吃的。

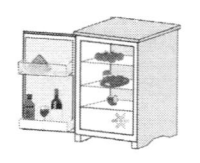

18

Find, circle, and write.

部首练习
Semantic Radicals

毛	铅	口	筷	花	足	跳	高
钢	笔	袋	子	篮	球	拍	手
琴	风	羽	毛	凉	鞋	网	斑
剑	筝	火	虫	绿	冰	骑	马
拉	弓	箭	老	树	箱	车	虎
门	前	剪	刀	林	割	草	机

1. 钢笔   2. _____   3. _____

4. _____   5. _____   6. _____

7. _____   8. _____   9. _____

10. _____   11. _____   12. _____

19

xiào
笑一笑. Learn these words and draw different kinds of smiling faces.

hā 哈哈大笑 laugh out loud	wēi 微微一笑 gentle and calm smile	méi 眉开眼笑 brows raised and eyes shining with delight
lù chǐ ér 露齿而笑 (with teeth shown) grin	diào 笑掉大牙 laugh one's teeth off	wān yāo 笑弯了腰 curled up with laughter (bend over one's waist)

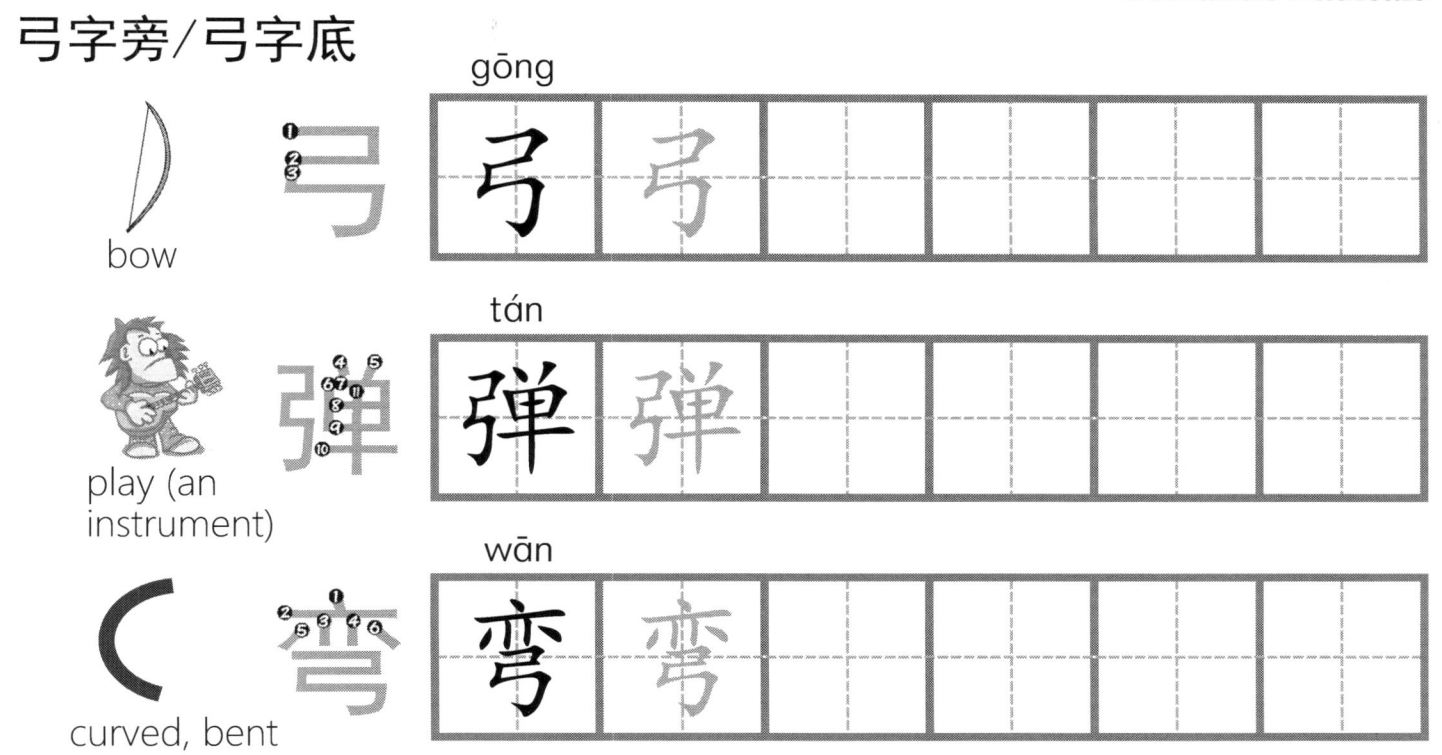

部首练习
Semantic Radicals

弓字旁/弓字底

gōng
弓 弓

bow

tán
弹 弹

play (an instrument)

wān
弯 弯

curved, bent

Find and trace 弓 in these characters.

lā
拉 弓
pull

弯 月

dì
弟 弟

qiáng
强 大
strong

ruò
弱 小
weak

弹 钢琴

jí
弹 吉他
guitar

Reduplication of an adjective (such as 弯弯的) makes the language more descriptive and poetic. Read this poem and underline all the reduplication structures in it (AA 的). Then use this structure to complete the other poems.

小小的船
(by 叶圣陶) shèng tāo

<u>弯弯的</u>月儿<u>小小的</u>船。

<u>小小的</u>船儿两头尖，

我在<u>小小的</u>船里坐，

只看见<u>闪闪的</u>星星<u>蓝蓝的</u>天。
（zhǐ 只 only / jiàn 见 see）

1. <u>青青的</u>草地，_____花，
   _____小路到我家。　（青　红　弯）
   (qīng green)

2. 我家有个小妹妹，
   _____眉毛，_____脸。
   _____眼睛对我看。　（长　红　弯）

3. _____天上_____云，
   白云那边有人家。　（蓝　白）
   _____小河<u>清清的</u>水，
   水里有鱼虾。　（弯　清）
   (qīng clear)

22

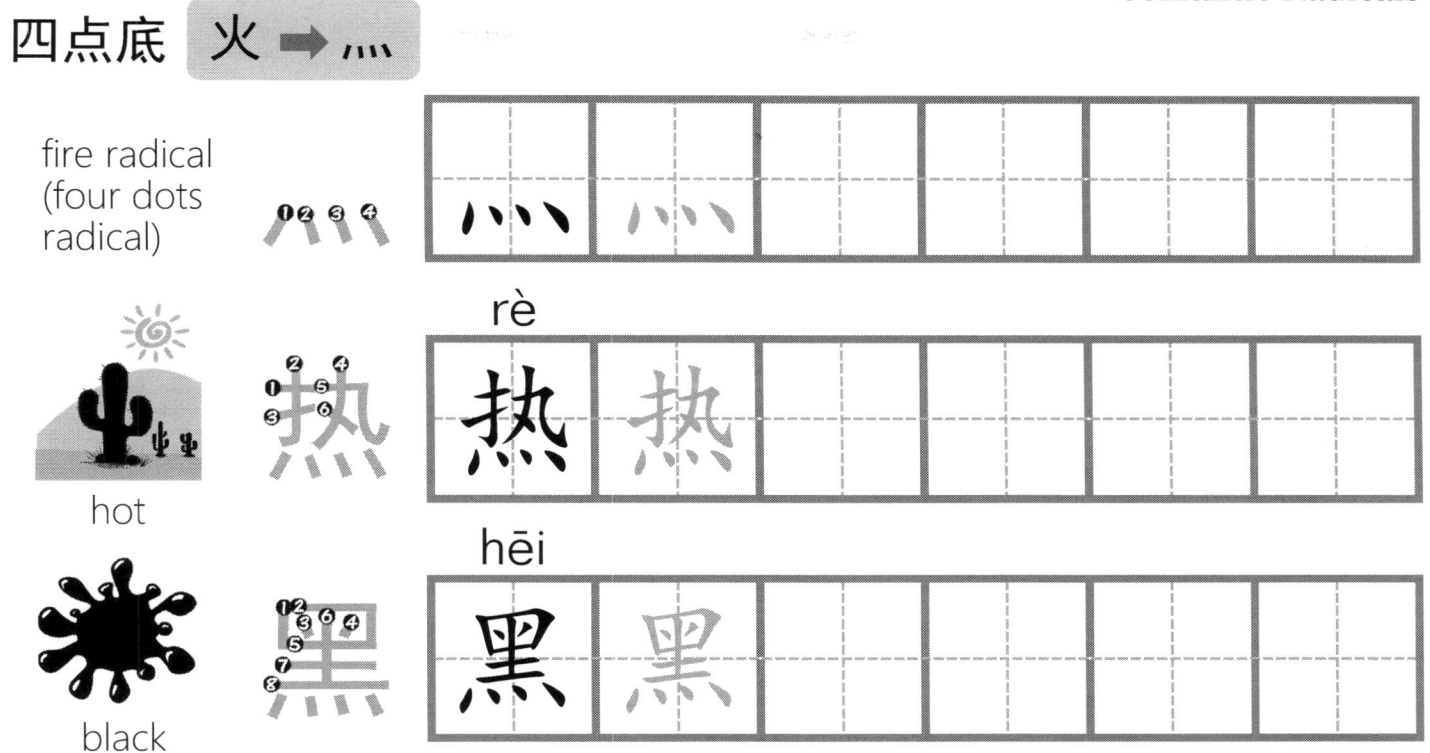

部首练习
Semantic Radicals

四点底 火 ➡ 灬

fire radical (four dots radical)

灬 灬

rè
热 热

hēi
黑 黑

Find and trace 灬 in these characters.

yè
黑夜
night

吃点心
dessert

zhào xiàng
照相
take a picture

zhǔ
煮鸡蛋
boil

rán
然后
then, next

shú
鸡蛋熟了
cooked, mature

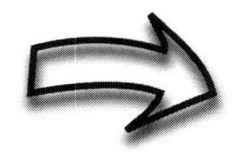

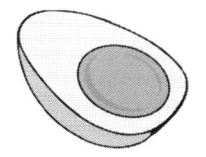

23

Make words with 热 and fill in the blanks.

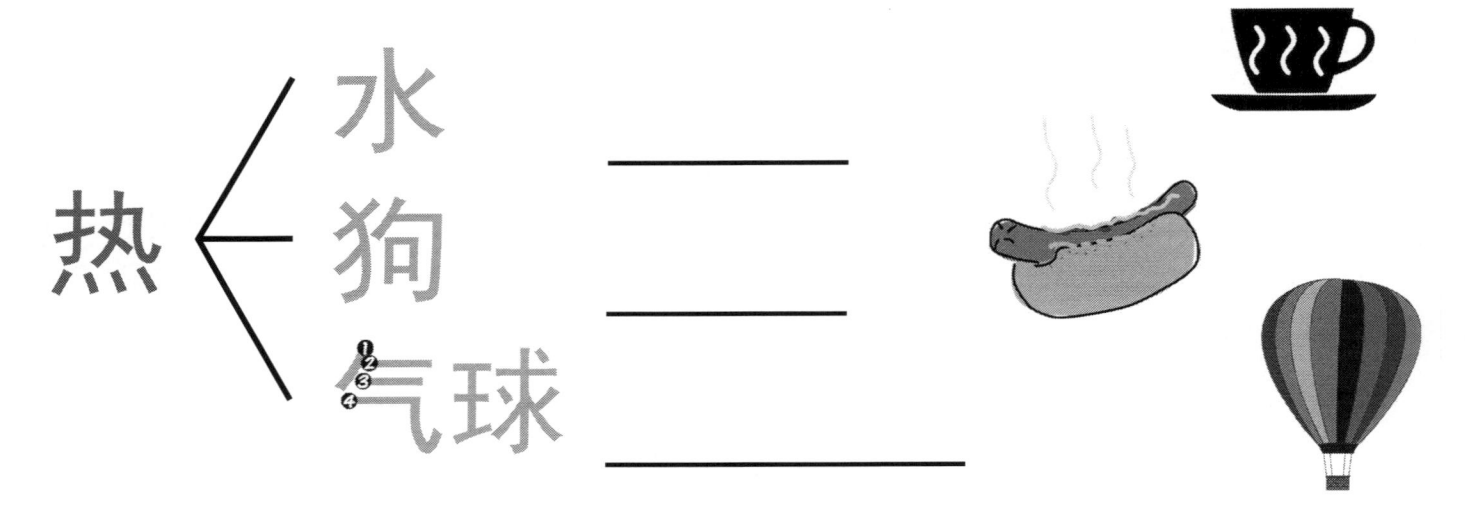

热 ← 水 _____
　　狗 _____
　　气球 _____

1. 美国人爱喝冷水，中国人爱喝_____。

2. 今天中午我在学校吃了_____。

3. 快看，_____飞上天了！

灬 is also used in characters for animals to represent their legs, wings, and/or tail. Add 灬 to these characters.

→ xióng
能
bear

能猫
panda

yàn
燕子
swallow

gāo
羊羔
lamb
(baby sheep)

24

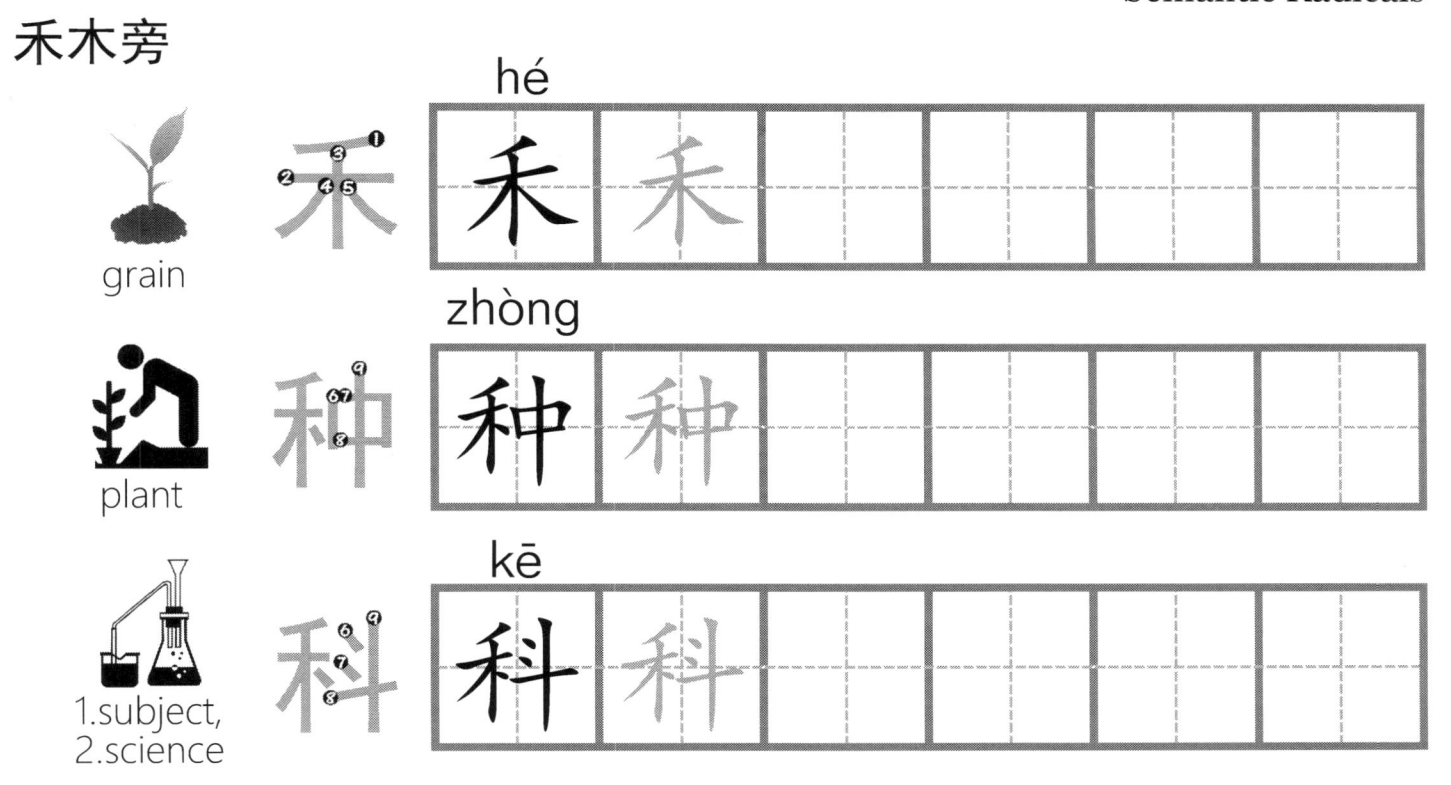

部首练习
Semantic Radicals

禾木旁

grain — 禾 — hé 禾 禾

plant — 种 — zhòng 种 种

1.subject, 2.science — 科 — kē 科 科

Find and trace 禾 in these characters.

zhòng
种树

zhǒng
种子
seed

miáo
禾苗
sprout

科学
science

科目
subject

秋天

miǎo
一秒钟
a second

25

Fill in the blanks with characters in the box.

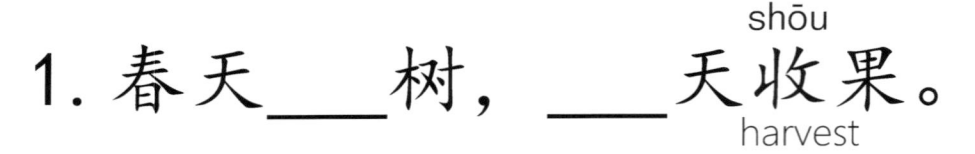

种　科　秒　秋　和

1. 春天___树，___天收果。

2. ___瓜得瓜，___豆得豆。

Plant melons and get melons. Plant beans and get beans. (You reap what you sow.)

3. 一分钟等于六十___钟。

4. 长大了，我要当___学家。

5. 科学___音乐都是我喜欢的科目。

Write down the time on the timer.

01 : 23 : 45　　一小时二十三分四十五秒

04 : 38 : 56　　_____

07 : 49 : 21　　_____

26

部首练习
Semantic Radicals

jiǎo sī
绞丝旁

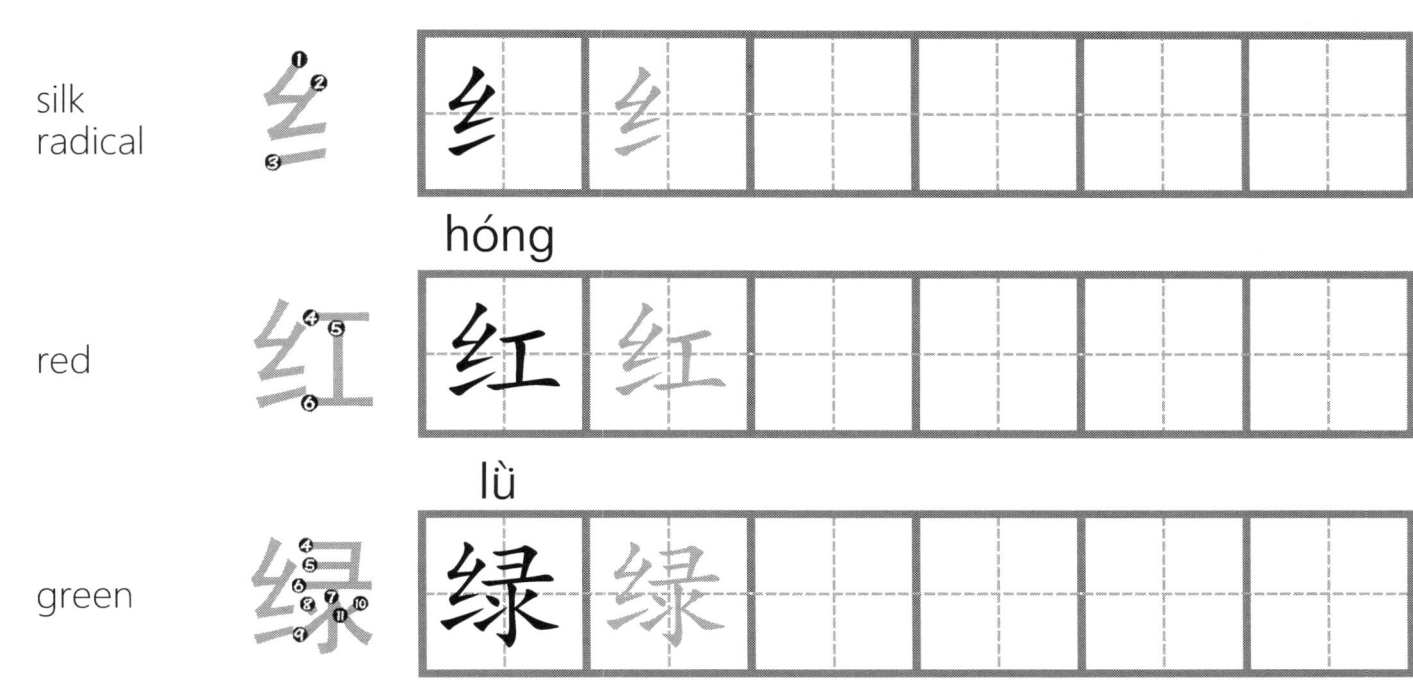

silk radical — 纟

hóng
red — 红

lǜ
green — 绿

Find and trace 纟 in these characters.

红绿灯
traffic light

hú dié jié
蝴蝶结
bow

bīng
结冰
freeze

jí
年级
grade

liàn xí
练习
practice

shéng
跳绳
jump rope

xiàn
毛线
yarn

斑马线
zebra crossing

27

Fill in the blanks with characters in the box.

| 练 | 红 | 级 | 结 | 绿 | 线 |

1. 放学后，我要____习写中文。

2. 冬天，河水___了冰。

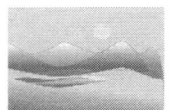

3. ___灯停，___灯行。
   (tíng stop) (xíng go)

4. 过马路要走斑马___。

5. 哥哥八岁，上三年___。

3rd Grade

6. 彩虹有七色：___、橙、黄、
   (hóng rainbow)
   ___、青、蓝、紫。
   (zǐ)

结绳记事 (jì shì) Before written language was invented, people kept records of events by tying knots on ropes. Try to tie the numbers 1-10 with some ropes.

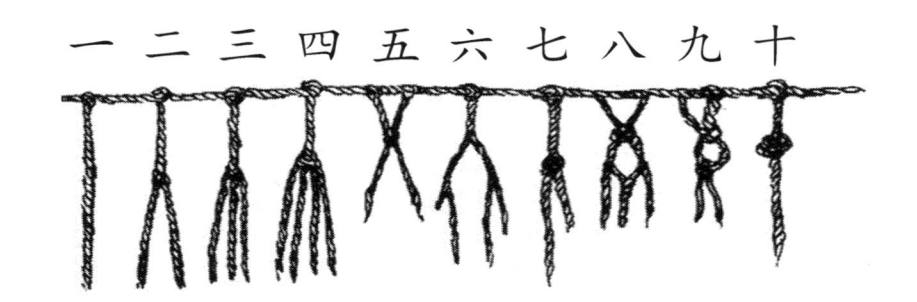

一 二 三 四 五 六 七 八 九 十

28

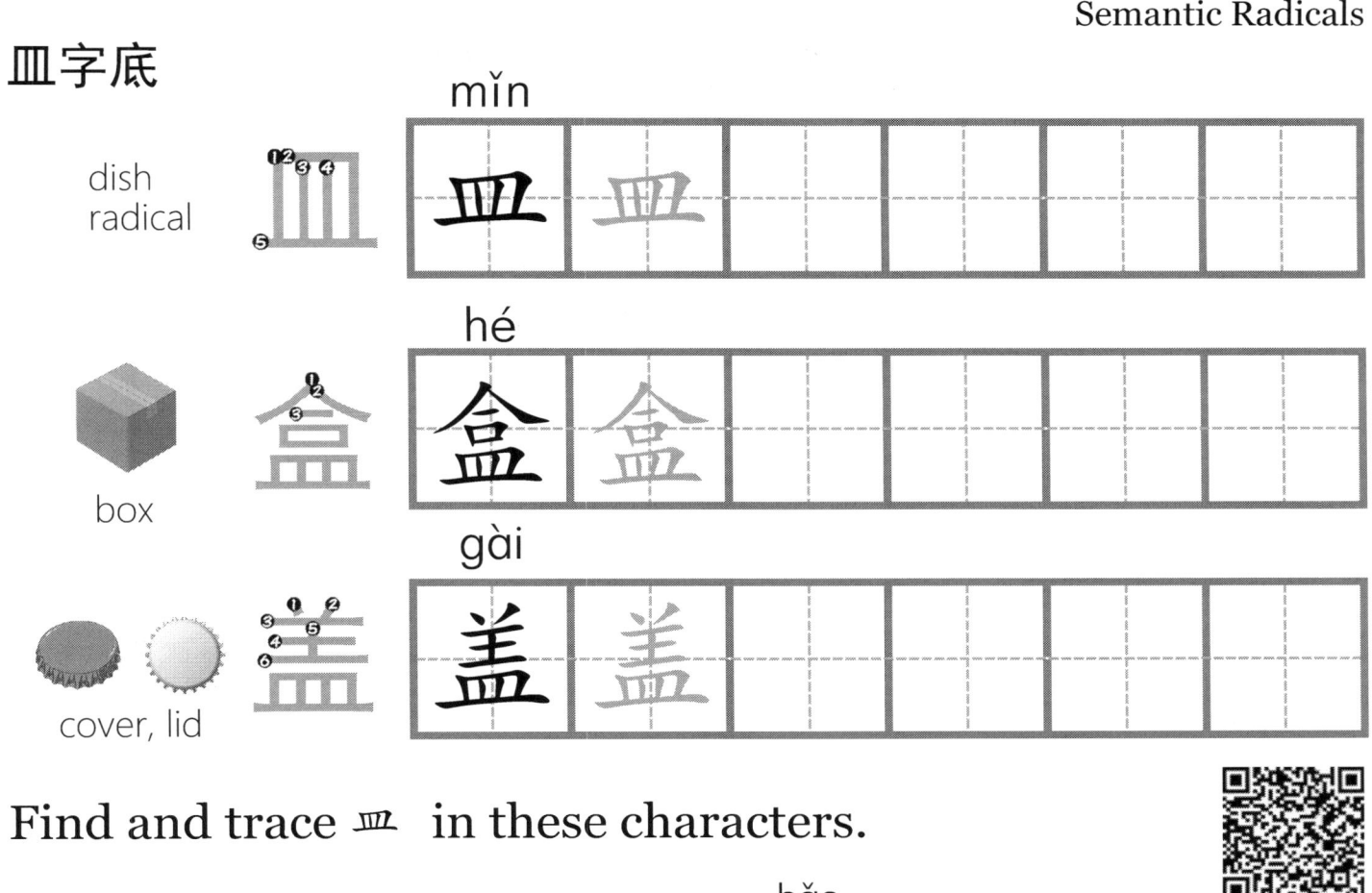

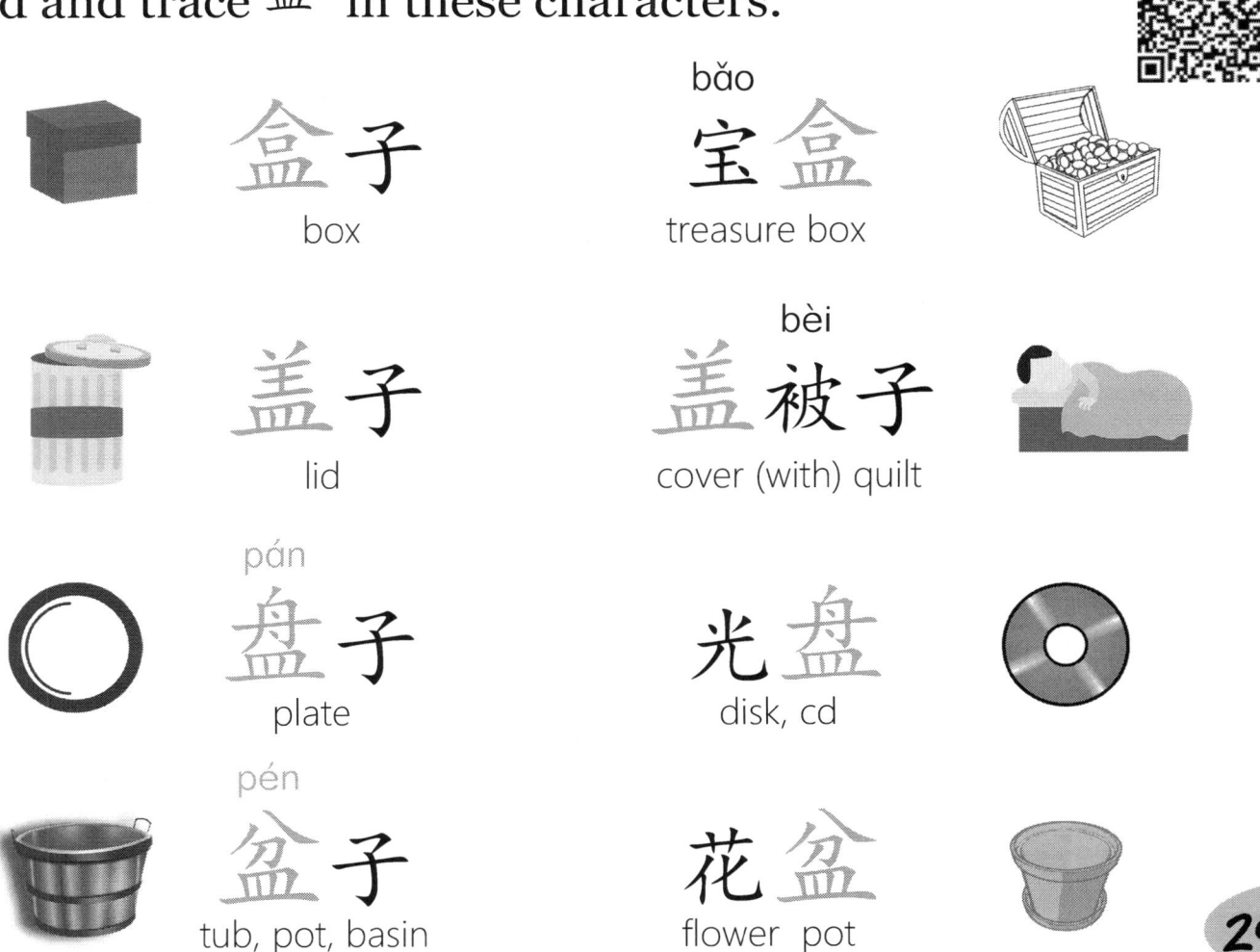

部首练习
Semantic Radicals

皿字底

dish radical — 皿 — mǐn — 皿 皿

box — 盒 — hé — 盒 盒

cover, lid — 盖 — gài — 盖 盖

Find and trace 皿 in these characters.

盒子 — box

宝盒 — bǎo — treasure box

盖子 — lid

盖被子 — bèi — cover (with) quilt

盘子 — pán — plate

光盘 — disk, cd

盆子 — pén — tub, pot, basin

花盆 — flower pot

29

Make words with 盒.

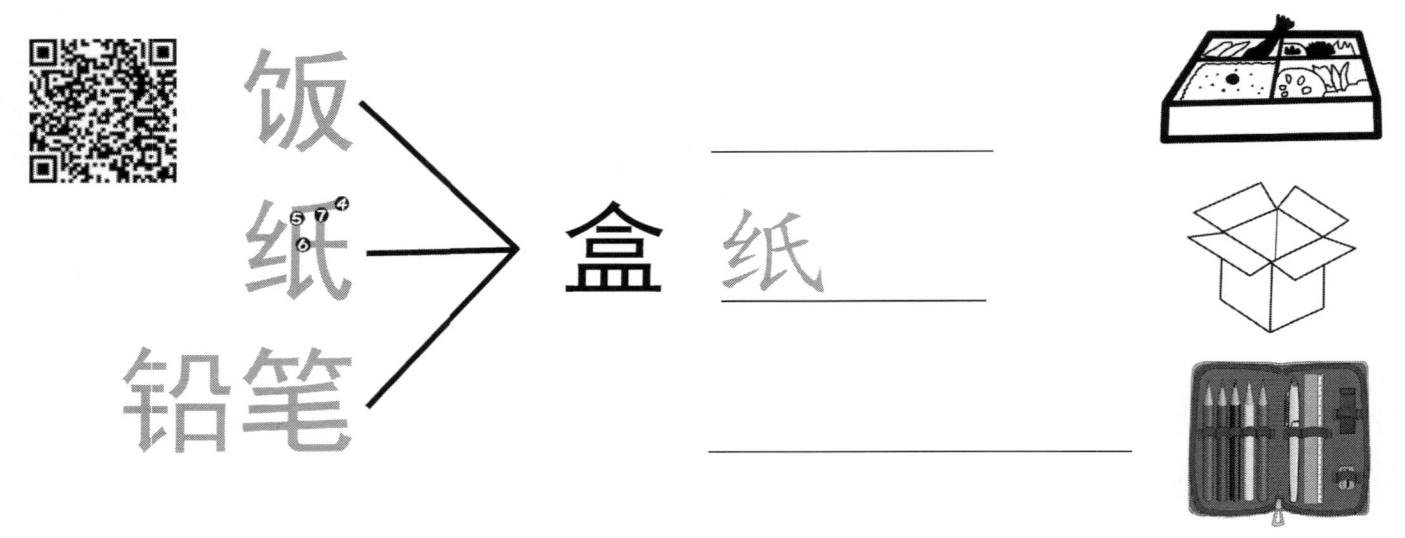

饭 ─┐
纸 ──→ 盒　纸 _____
铅笔 ─┘　　　_____
　　　　　　　_____

Read and draw.

1. 铅笔盒里有铅笔、橡皮和剪刀。
   　　　　　　　　　　xiàng

2. 饭盒里有虾、鸡腿、米饭和青菜。
   　　　　　　tuǐ　　　　qīng cài
   　　　　chicken leg　green veggies

30

月字旁/月字底　肉 ➡ 月

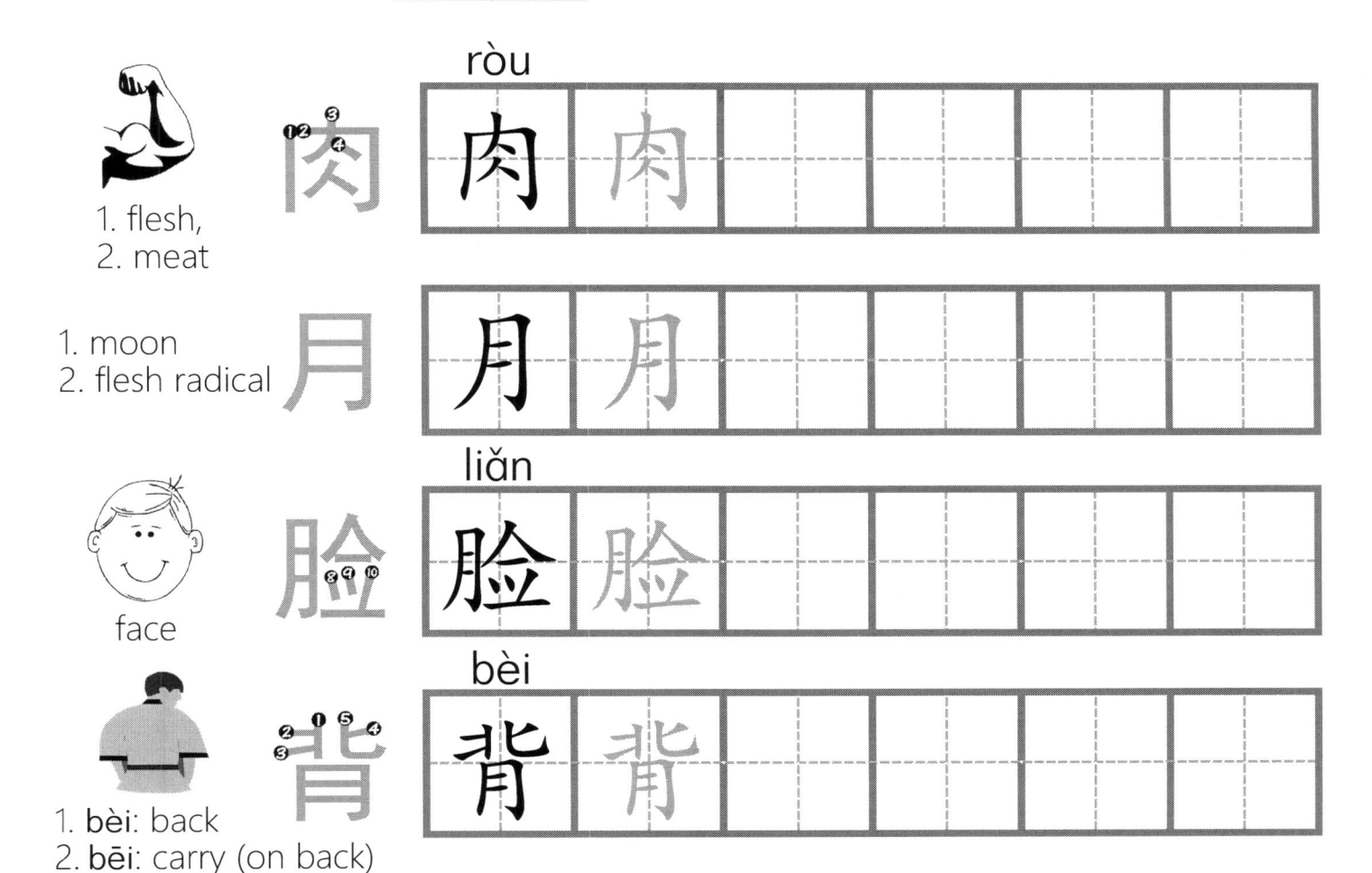

部首练习
Semantic Radicals

1. flesh,
2. meat

ròu
肉 肉

1. moon
2. flesh radical

月 月

face

liǎn
脸 脸

1. bèi: back
2. bēi: carry (on back)

bèi
背 背

Find and trace 月 in these words. Then cut out the shapes and paste them on the next page.

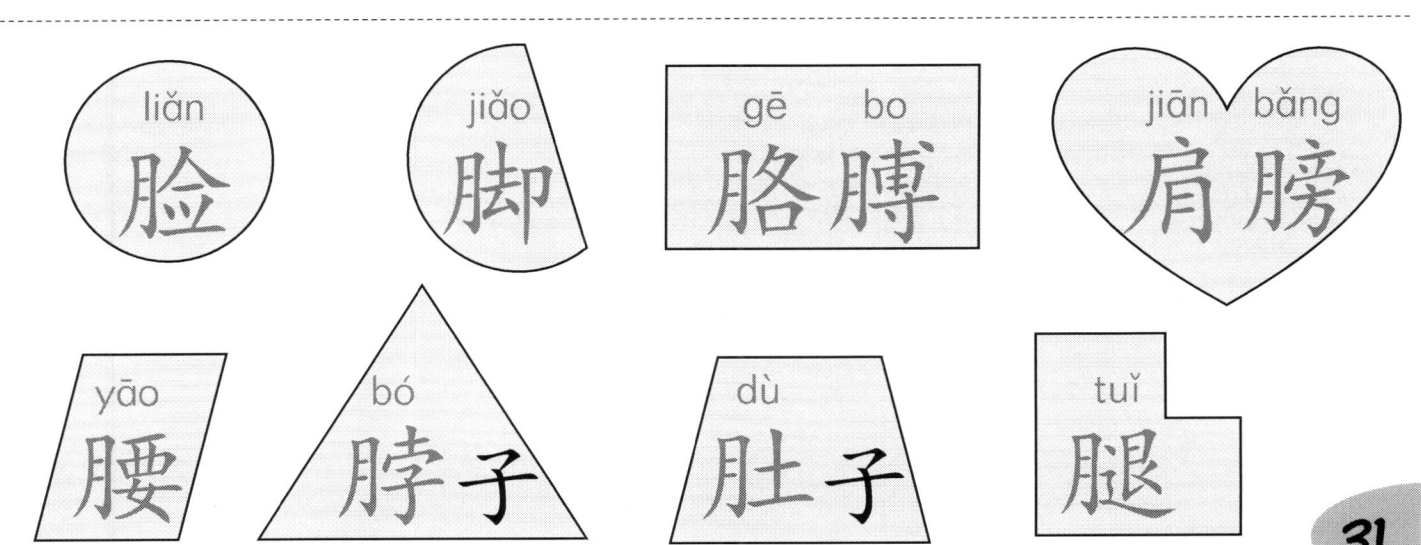

liǎn
脸

jiǎo
脚

gē bo
胳膊

jiān bǎng
肩膀

yāo
腰

bó
脖子

dù
肚子

tuǐ
腿

31

Paste your words on this page. Then draw a line from the words to the body parts.

face

neck

arm

shoulder

belly

waist

foot

leg

32

部首练习
Semantic Radicals

Fill in the blanks with characters in the box.

脖　脸　背　脚　肚

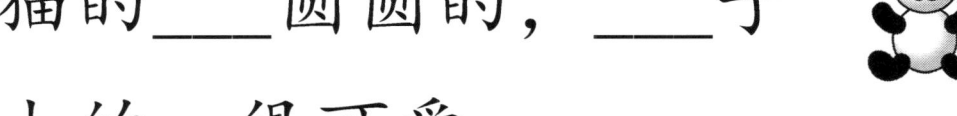

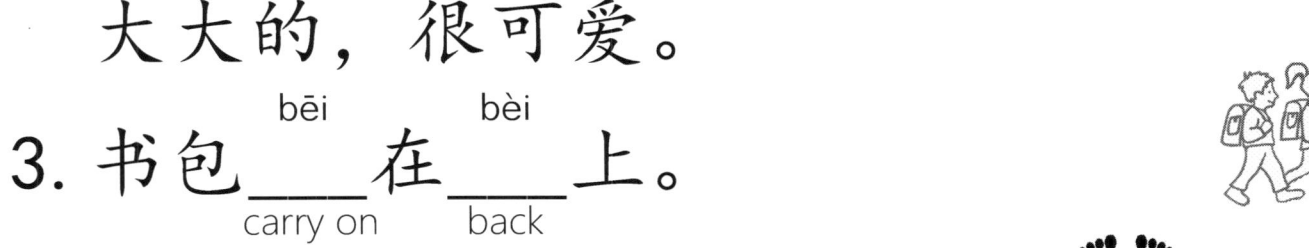

1. 长颈鹿的___子长。
2. 熊猫的___(yuán)圆圆的，___子大大的，很可爱。
3. 书包___(bēi)在___(bèi)上。
   　　carry on　　back
4. 大口吃四方，大___走天下。

Read and trace 月 in more characters.

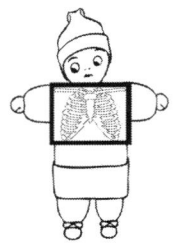

péng　you
朋　友

zāng　　fu
脏　衣服
dirty　clothes

gǔ
骨头
bone

dǎn　　rú　shǔ
胆小如鼠
coward as a mouse

33

Human organs.

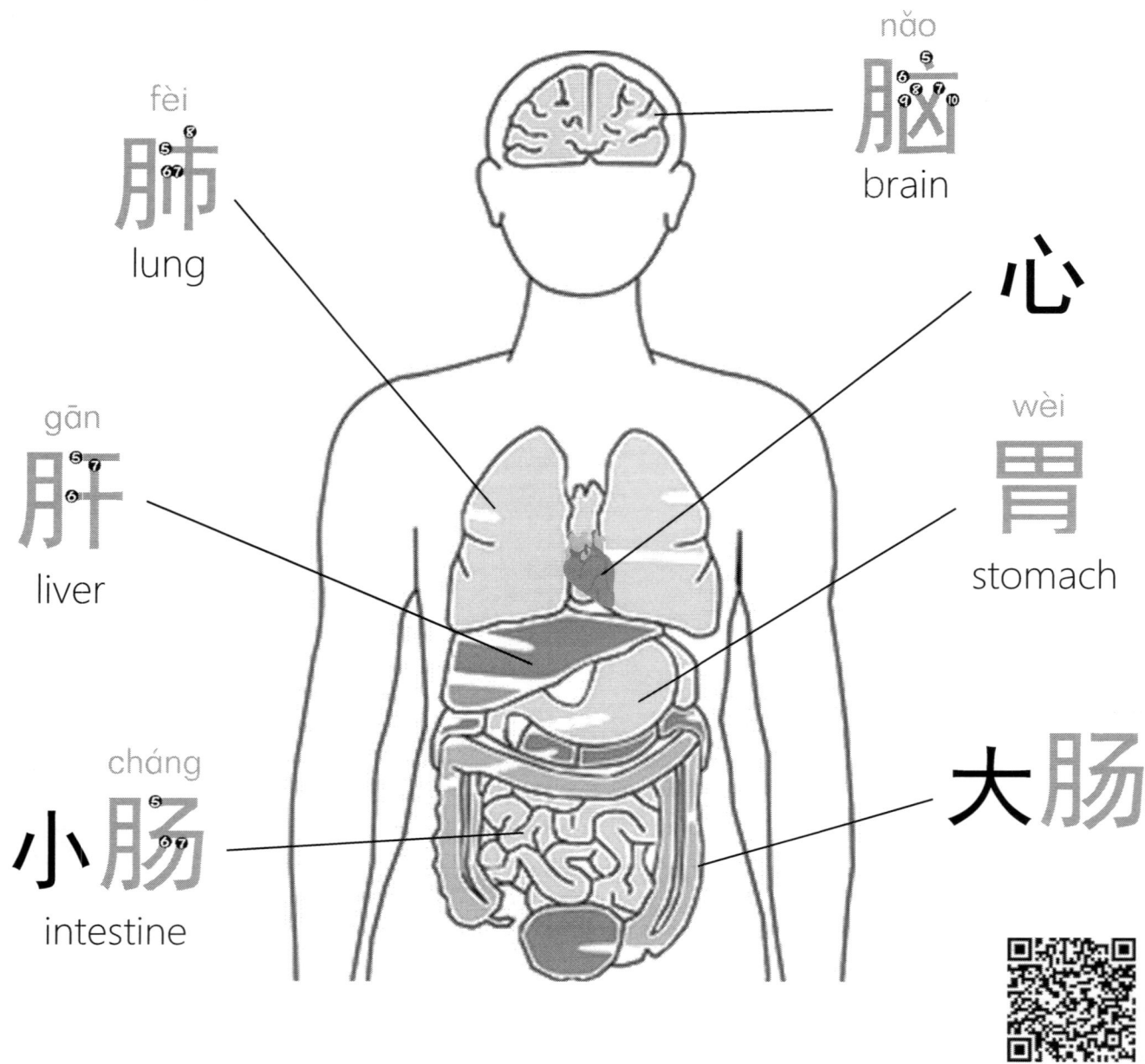

nǎo
脑
brain

fèi
肺
lung

心

gān
肝
liver

wèi
胃
stomach

cháng
小肠
intestine

大肠

Can you write down the name for each organ?

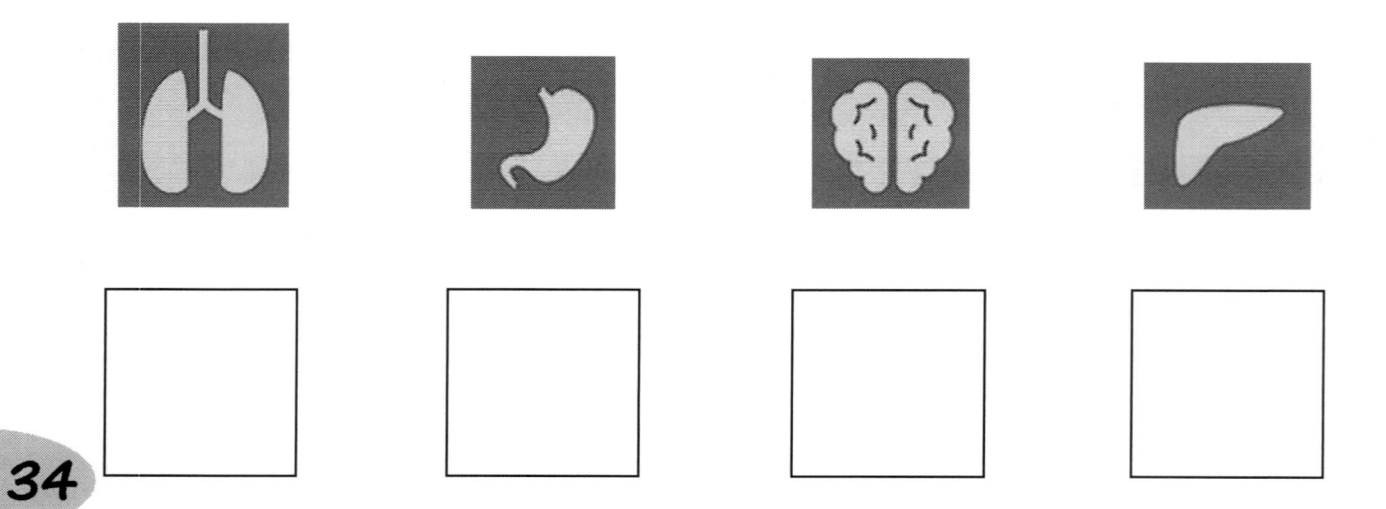

34

部首练习
Semantic Radicals

心字底

heart — xīn 心

you (formal, courteous) — nín 您

forget — wàng 忘

Find and trace 心 in these characters.

您好
hello

bié
别忘了
don't forget

休息

zháo jí
着急
anxious

yì si
意思
meaning

gù
故意
on purpose

xiǎng
想一想
think about it

gǎn xiè
感谢

ēn jié
感恩节
Thanksgiving

35

Fill in the blanks with characters in the box.

| 想 | 意 | 急 | 思 | 忘 |
| 您 | 息 | 感 | 恩 | |

1. 别着___，慢慢来。
   (màn)
   take your time

2. 对不起，我___了今天是星期一。
   (duì) sorry

3. ___一___，上小下大是什么字？

4. 这个字是什么_____？

5. ___ ___节，美国人都吃火鸡。

6. 我们从星期一到星期五上学，星期六和星期天休___。

7. ___好！想喝点儿什么？

shù
竖心旁   心 ➡ 忄

部首练习
Semantic Radicals

vertical heart radical

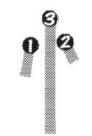

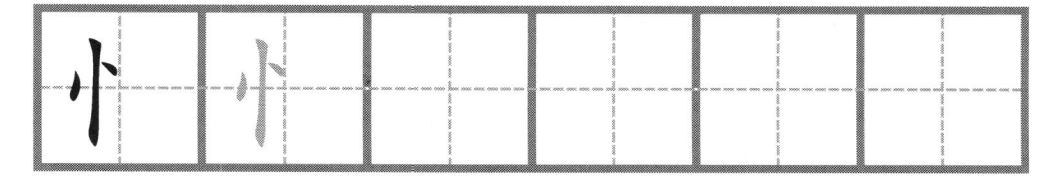

忄 忄

pà
怕 怕

afraid, scared

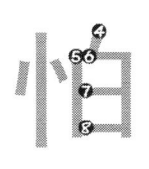

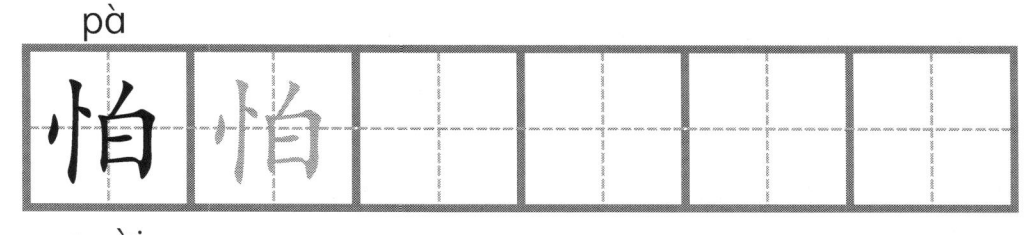

guài
怪 怪

1. strange
2. to blame

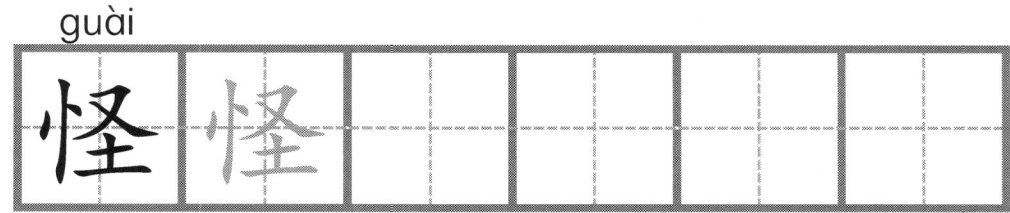

Find and trace 忄 in these characters.

kuài lè
快乐
happy

gǎn
赶快
hurry

máng lù
忙碌
busy

jīng
吃惊
surprised

qí
奇怪
strange, weird

wù
怪物
monster

别怪我
don't blame me

dǒng
懂了
understood

kě lián
可怜
poor, pitiful

37

Fill in the blanks with characters in the box.

| 怪 | 快 | 怜 | 怕 | 忙 |

1. 两只老虎跑得___，一只没有耳朵，一只没有尾巴，真奇___。

2. 奶奶不喜欢冬天，因为她___冷。

3. 爸爸每天都很___，没有时间和我玩。

4. 小猫找不到妈妈了，它好可___。
   (very)

Substitute the radical to make another character and then use it in a word.

怕 + 扌 ➡ __ (　　)

怜 + 钅 ➡ __ (　　)

快 + 土 ➡ __ (　　)

忙 + 心 ➡ __ (　　)

惊 + 冫 ➡ __ (　　)

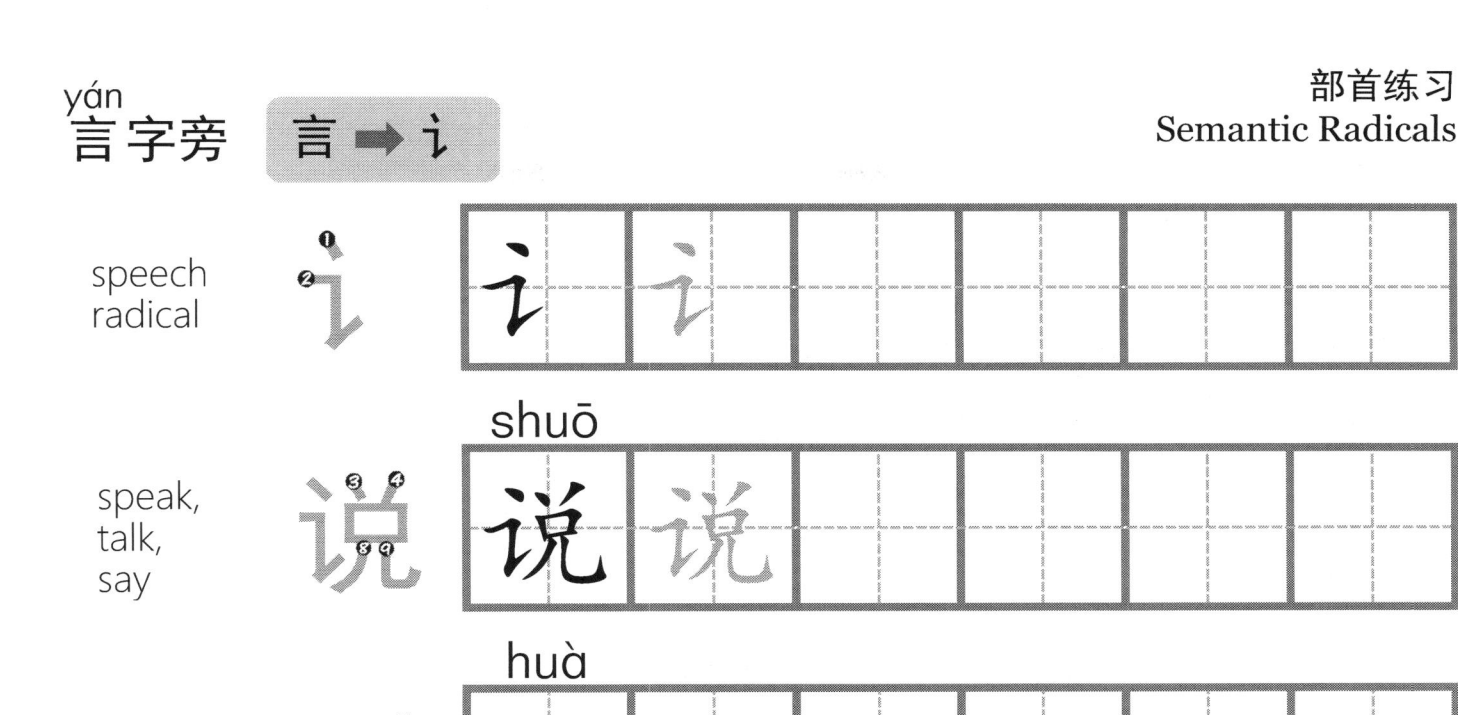

部首练习
Semantic Radicals

yán
言字旁   言 ➡ 讠

speech radical   讠

shuō
说   speak, talk, say

huà
话   spoken words

Find and trace 讠 in these characters.

说话
talk

yǔ yán
语言
language

kè
上课
attend class

qǐng
请坐
please sit down

xiè
谢谢

ràng
让路

rèn shi
认识
know, recognize

zhēn
认真
serious, earnest

39

Fill in the blanks with characters in the box.

| 请 | 让 | 认识 | 语 | 说 | 话 |

1. 你会___什么语言？
   我会说英___和汉___。
   　　　English　　Chinese

2. 你_____这个字吗？

3. 汽车停下来给行人___路。
   　　stop

4. ___进！___坐！___喝茶！
   come in　　　　　　have some tea

5. 救火车来了，快___开。
   fire truck

6. 我不_____你，我不跟你走！

7. 有事___给我打电___。
   If you need anything, give me a call.

40

部首练习
Semantic Radicals

双人旁

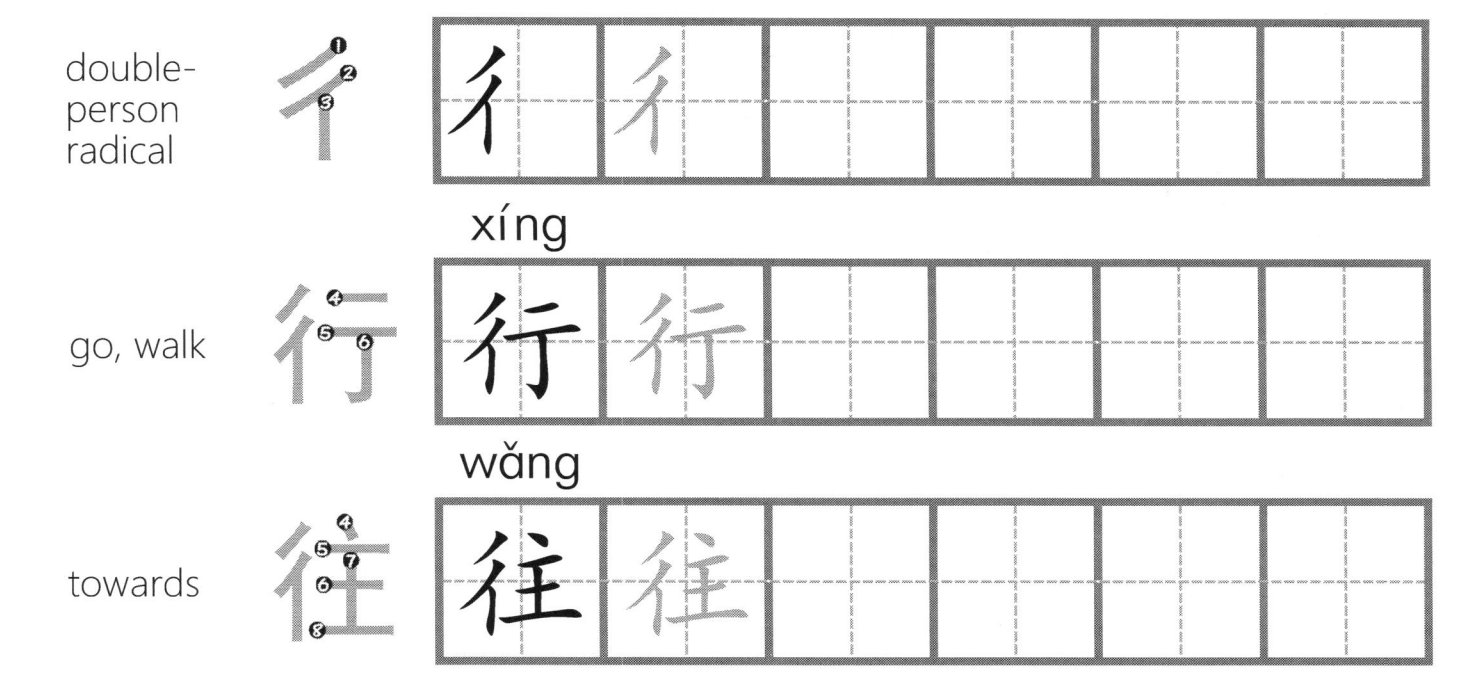

double-person radical 彳

go, walk xíng 行

towards wǎng 往

Find and trace 彳 in these characters.

行人
pedestrian

人行道
dào
sidewalk

旅行
lǔ
travel

往前看
look forward

纪律
jì lǜ
discipline

很好
hěn
very good

得到
dé
receive, get

微风
wēi
(slight) breeze

微笑
smile

41

Fill in the blanks with 停. Then read and memorize this chart.

九九乘法表
chéng fǎ biǎo

一一得一								
一二得二	二二得四							
一三三	二三_六	三三_九						
一四得四	二四_八	三四十二	四四十六					
一五_五	二五一十	三五十五	四五二十	五五二十五				
一六得六	二六十二	三六十八	四六二十四	五六三十	六六三十六			
一七_七	二七十四	三七二十一	四七二十八	五七三十五	六七四十二	七七四十九		
一八得八	二八十六	三八二十四	四八三十二	五八四十	六八四十八	七八五十六	八八六十四	
一九_九	二九十八	三九二十七	四九三十六	五九四十五	六九五十四	七九六十三	八九七十二	九九八十一

42

Use the chart above to finish these multiplication sentences.

1×1=								
1×2=	2×2=							
1×3=	2×3=	3×3=						
1×4=	2×4=	3×4=	4×4=					
1×5=	2×5=	3×5=	4×5=	5×5=				
1×6=	2×6=	3×6=	4×6=	5×6=	6×6=			
1×7=	2×7=	3×7=	4×7=	5×7=	6×7=	7×7=		
1×8=	2×8=	3×8=	4×8=	5×8=	6×8=	7×8=	8×8=	
1×9=	2×9=	3×9=	4×9=	5×9=	6×9=	7×9=	8×9=	9×9=

43

Find, circle, and write.

雪	人	上	课	看	书	日	星
自	行	车	后	口	包	光	盘
弯	道	吃	惊	红	绿	灯	盐
奇	怪	饭	盒	腿	花	耳	环
动	物	毛	洗	脚	盆	朵	可
斑	马	线	脸	脏	手	快	乐

1. 人行道
2. _____
3. _____
4. _____
5. _____
6. _____
7. _____
8. _____
9. _____
10. _____

部首练习
Semantic Radicals

走之底 之 ➡ 辶

横折折撇
(stroke)

walk
radical

zhè
this,
here
这

Find and trace 辶 in these characters.

这里
here

páng biān
旁边
next to

guò
过马路
cross the road

yóu dì yuán
邮递员
postman

sòng xìn
送信
deliver mail

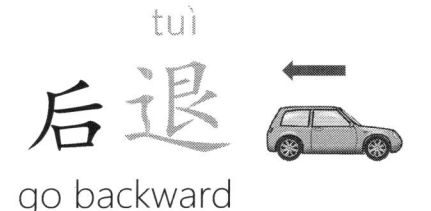

zhī
知道
know

jìn
前进
go forward

tuì
后退
go backward

chí
迟到
late

45

家庭纪律游戏棋 Home Rules Board Game
tíng jì lù yóu xì qí

两人玩
2 players

You'll need:

1. A die   2. Two pawns
   (you may use any small objects)

How to play:

1. Each player puts their pawn at the starting point.
2. Roll the die and read aloud the number on the die.
3. Move the number of steps indicated by the die. For example, if the player rolls a 4, the pawn moves 4 steps.
4. If the pawn lands on a spot with words, read it aloud, and follow the instructions.
5. The first one to reach the finish line wins!

xiě wán zuò yè jìn gé 写 完 作 业 进 两 格	"You've finished your homework." Move 2 spots forward.
tíng cì 玩手机 停 一 次	"You play (too much) cell phone." Lose a turn.
wù 做家务 进 三 格	"You help with housework." Move 3 spots forward.
tài táng tuì 吃 太 多 糖 退 两 格	"You eat too much candy." Move 2 spots back.
lián 学中文 连 一 次	"You study Chinese." Get a bonus turn.
qiǎng jù 抢 玩具 退 三 格	"You fight over toys." Move 3 spots back.

46

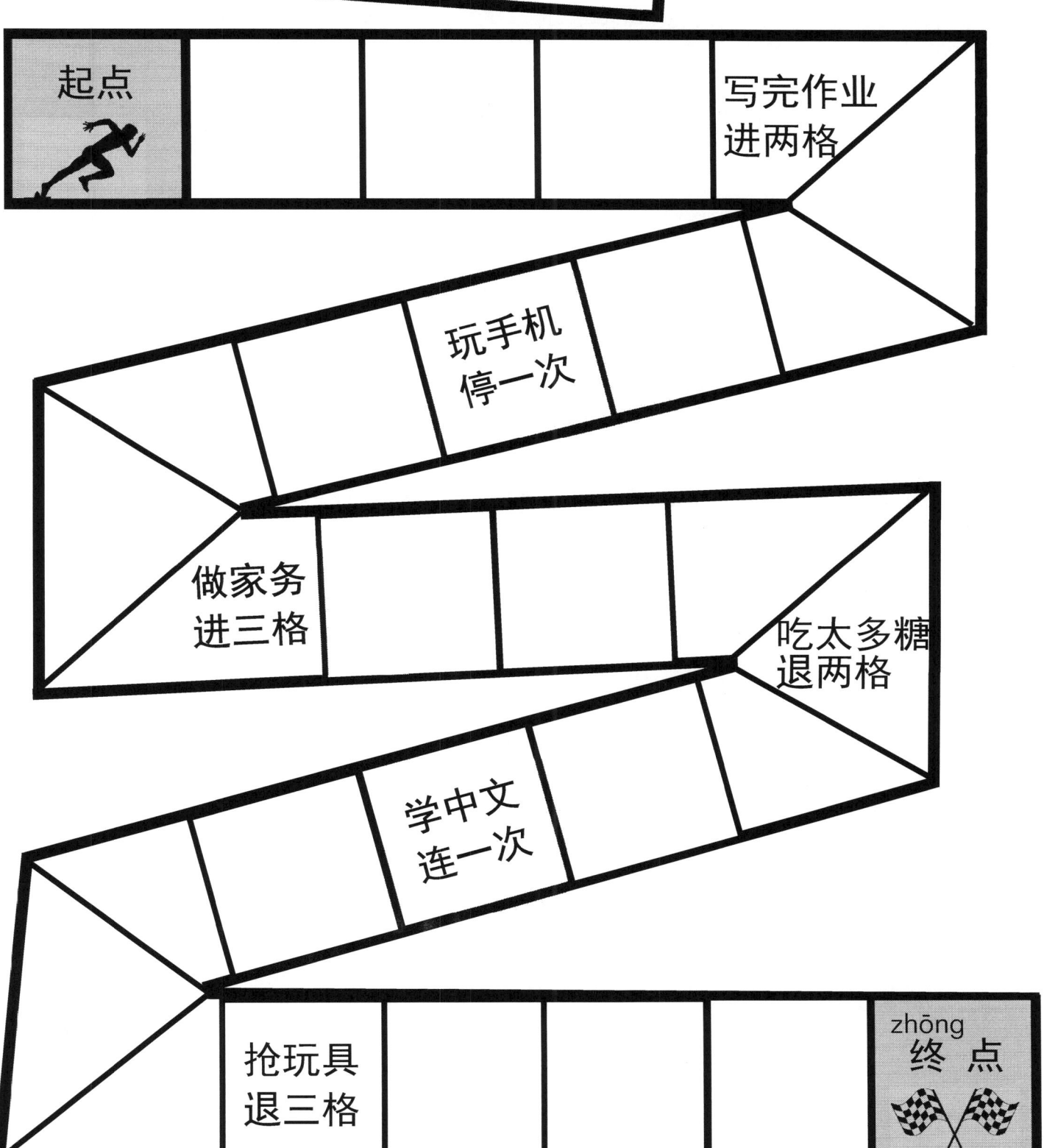

部首练习
Semantic Radicals

游戏棋

起点

写完作业
进两格

玩手机
停一次

做家务
进三格

吃太多糖
退两格

学中文
连一次

抢玩具
退三格

zhōng
终 点

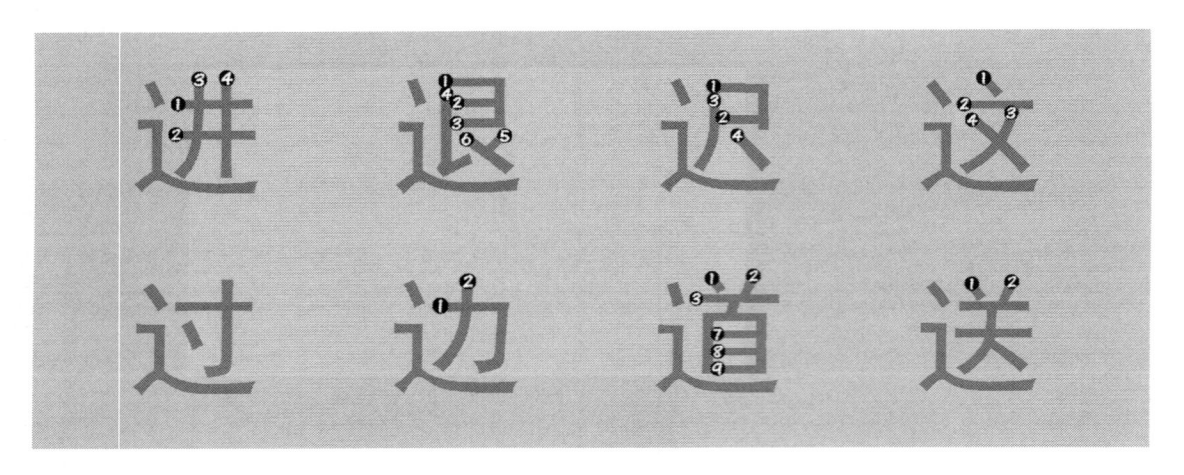

Fill in the blanks with characters in the box.

| 进 | 退 | 迟 | 这 |
| 过 | 边 | 道 | 送 |

1. ___马路要走斑马线。

2. ___是点点，他是我的好朋友。

3. 对不起，我___到了。

4. 邮递员(yóu dì yuán)每天下午三点来___信。

5. 马路的两___都是大树。

6. 虚心(xū shǐ)使人___步(bù)，骄傲(jiāo ào)使人落后。
Modesty helps one go forward.   Conceit makes one lag behind.

7. 你知___"虚心"的意思吗？

8. 看到熊，不能(néng)跑，要慢慢(màn)往后___。
cannot   slowly

部首练习
Semantic Radicals

fǎn
反文旁   文 ➡ 攵

hand movement radical — 攵

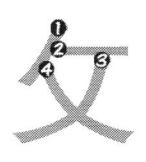

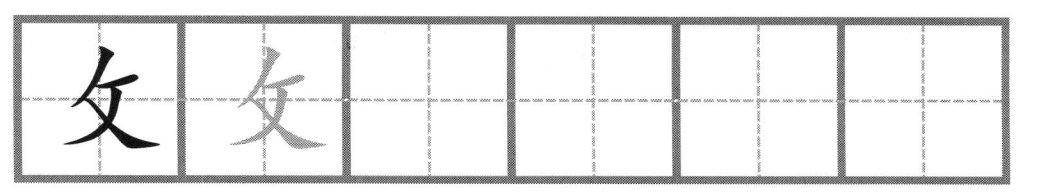

shōu — 收
gather, receive

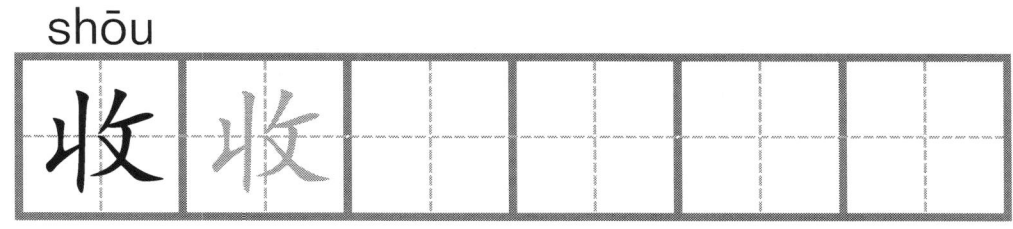

fàng — 放
1. put, place, 2. release

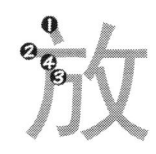

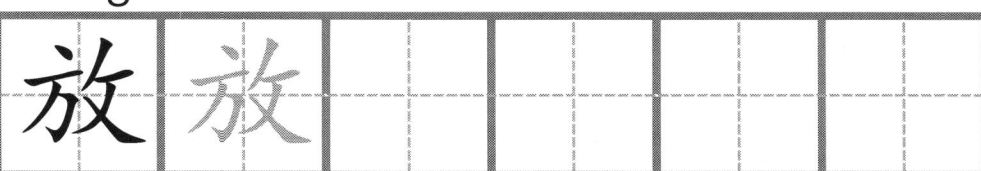

Find and trace 攵 in these characters.

huí
回收
recycle

xué
放学
school is over

shù
数学
Math

shǔ shù
数数
count numbers

gù shi
故事
story

yǒng gǎn
勇敢
brave

jiù mìng
救命
help (save life)

救生衣
life jacket

49

Fill in the blanks with characters in the box.

| 收 | 放 | 敢 | 数 | 救 |

1. 请把茶杯___到桌子上。

2. 请把玩具___起来。

3. 妹妹怕黑，不___一个人睡。

4. 睡不着，就躺在床上___羊。
   (tǎng) (lying)

5. 科学和___学都是我喜欢的科目。

6. 春天种树，秋天___果。

7. 明天___学后我要去划船。

8. 上船前，每个人都穿上___生衣。
   before boarding the boat

9. 小鸟不怕人，___来吃东西。

10. ___命啊！有人落水了！

50

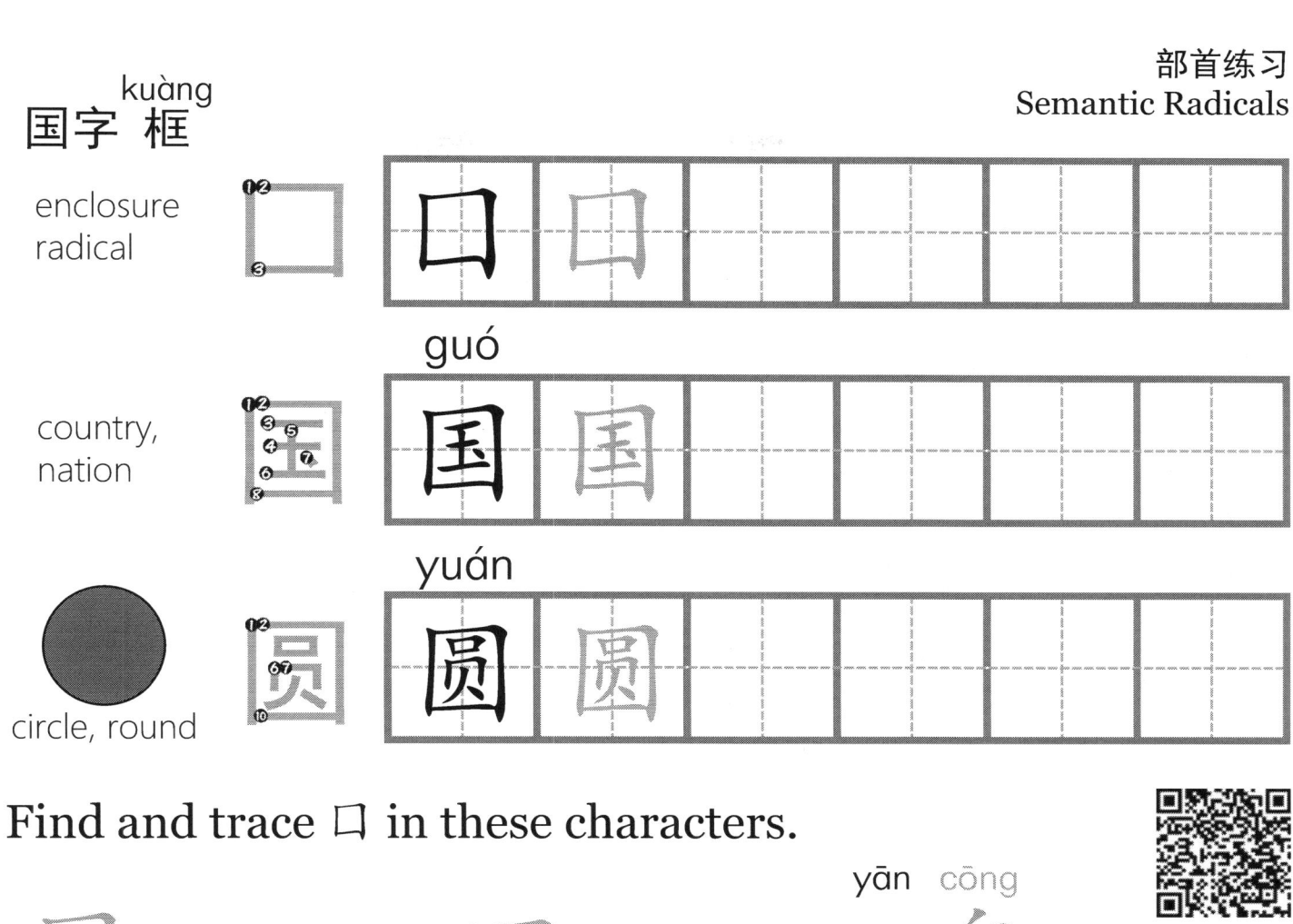

部首练习
Semantic Radicals

国字框 kuàng

enclosure radical

口 口

guó

country, nation

国 国

yuán

circle, round

圆 圆

Find and trace 口 in these characters.

国家
country

回家

烟囱 yān cōng
chimney

公园 yuán
park

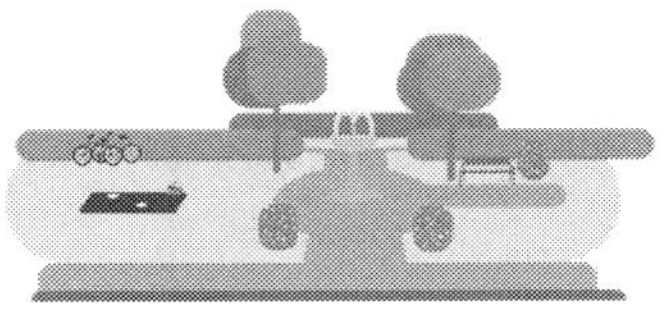

地图 tú
map

圆圈 quān
circle

围巾 wéi jīn
scarf

因为
because

Make words with 国 and fill in the blanks.

国 ← 家　王　歌

___家

___王

___歌

1. 我爱我的_____。

2. _____的女儿是公主。
   　　　　daughter　princess
   (zhǔ above 主)

3. 每天早上小学生们都要唱_____。

你生活在哪个国家？Circle the word for your country and color it on the map. (Label it in your own language if it's not listed here.)

中国
China

俄罗斯
é luó sī
Russia

印度
yìn dù
India

日本
běn
Japan

美国
United States

加拿大
Canada

墨西哥
mò
Mexico

澳大利亚
ào lì yà
Australia

英国
yīng
England

法国
fǎ
France

德国
dé
Germany

西班牙
bān
Spain

52

shì jiè
世界地图 World Map

左耳旁

left ear radical

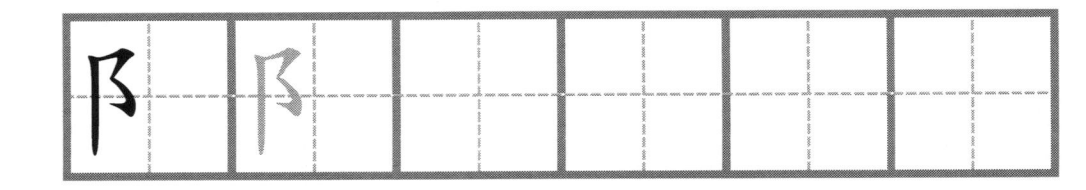

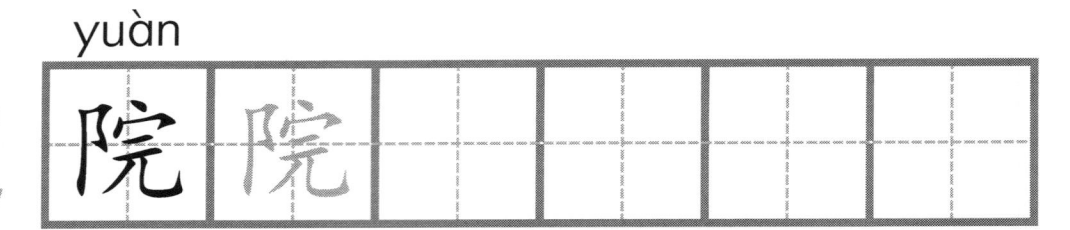

yuàn
yard

阝
院

Find and trace 阝 in these characters.

yī
医院

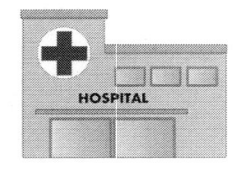

pái duì
排队

suí
跟随
follow

biàn
随便
casual, random

mò
陌生人
stranger

xiāo fáng yuán
消防员
firefighter

wēi xiǎn
危险
dangerous

chú
除法 ÷
division

chéng
加减乘除

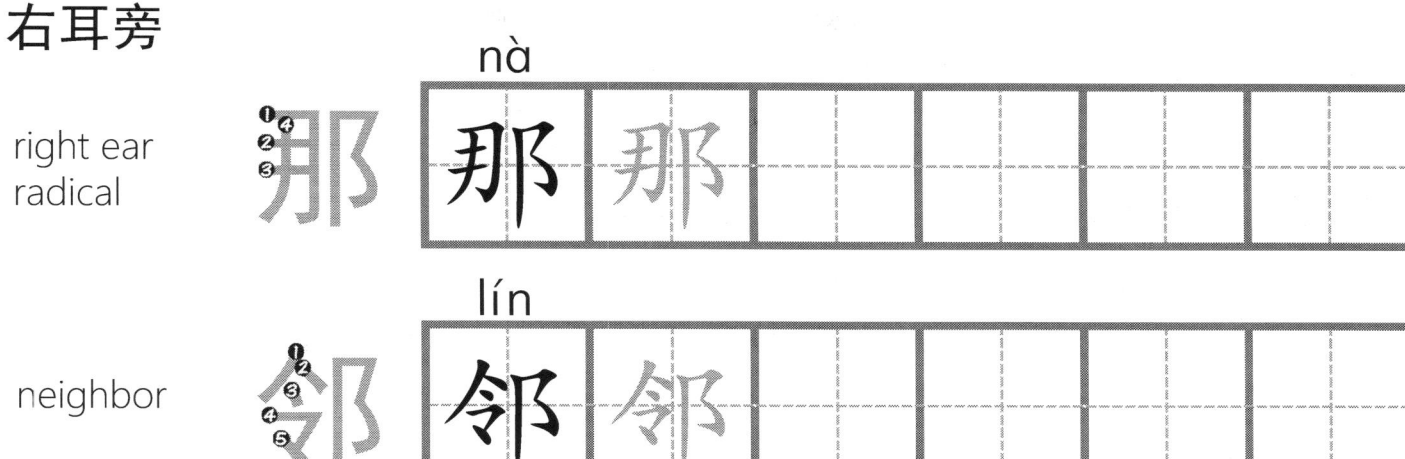

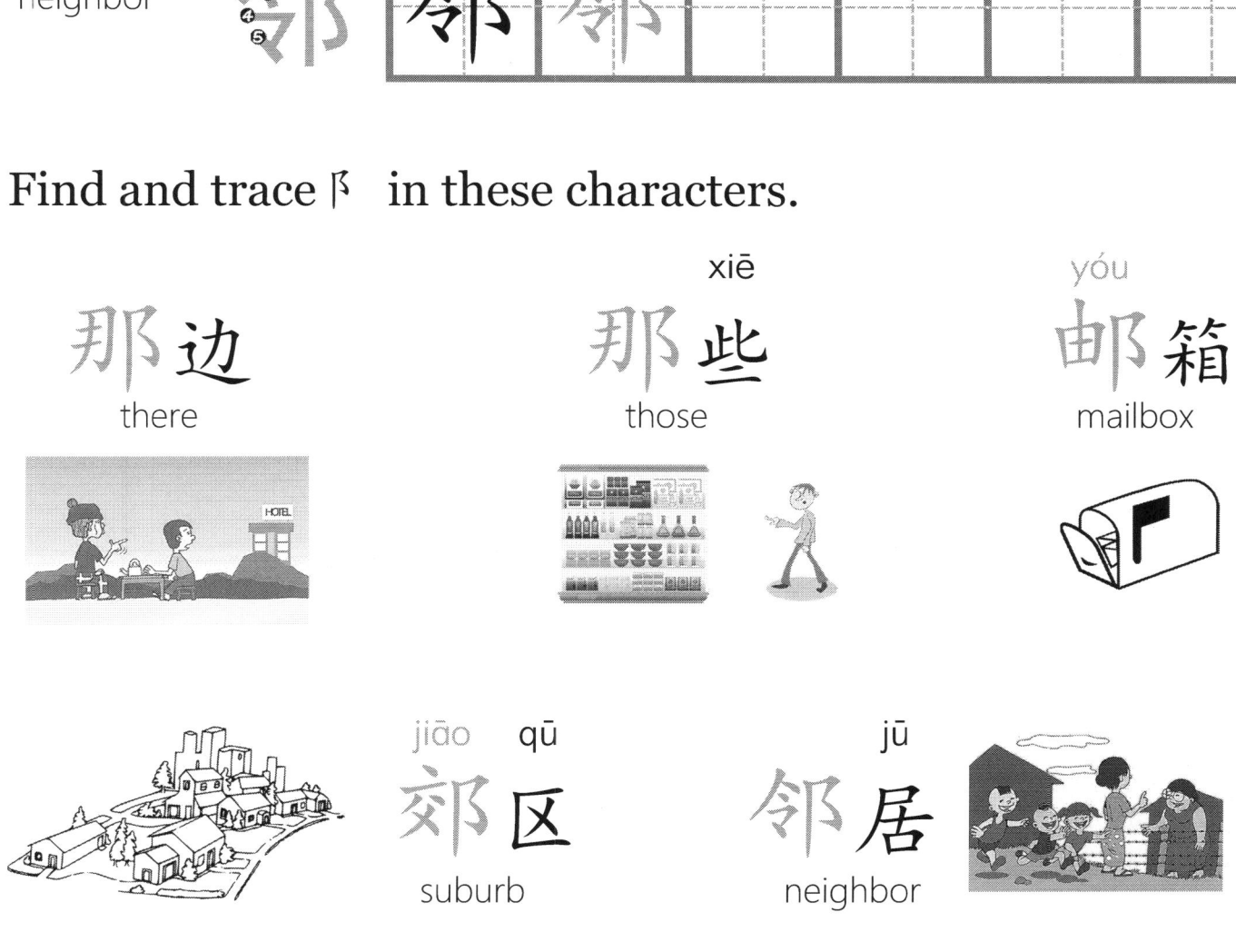

部首练习
Semantic Radicals

右耳旁

right ear radical

nà
那 那

lín
neighbor
邻 邻

Find and trace 阝 in these characters.

那边
there

xiē
那些
those

yóu
邮箱
mailbox

jiāo qū
郊区
suburb

jū
邻居
neighbor

shè
左邻右舍
neighbors next door

55

Substitute the radical to make another character and then use it in a word.

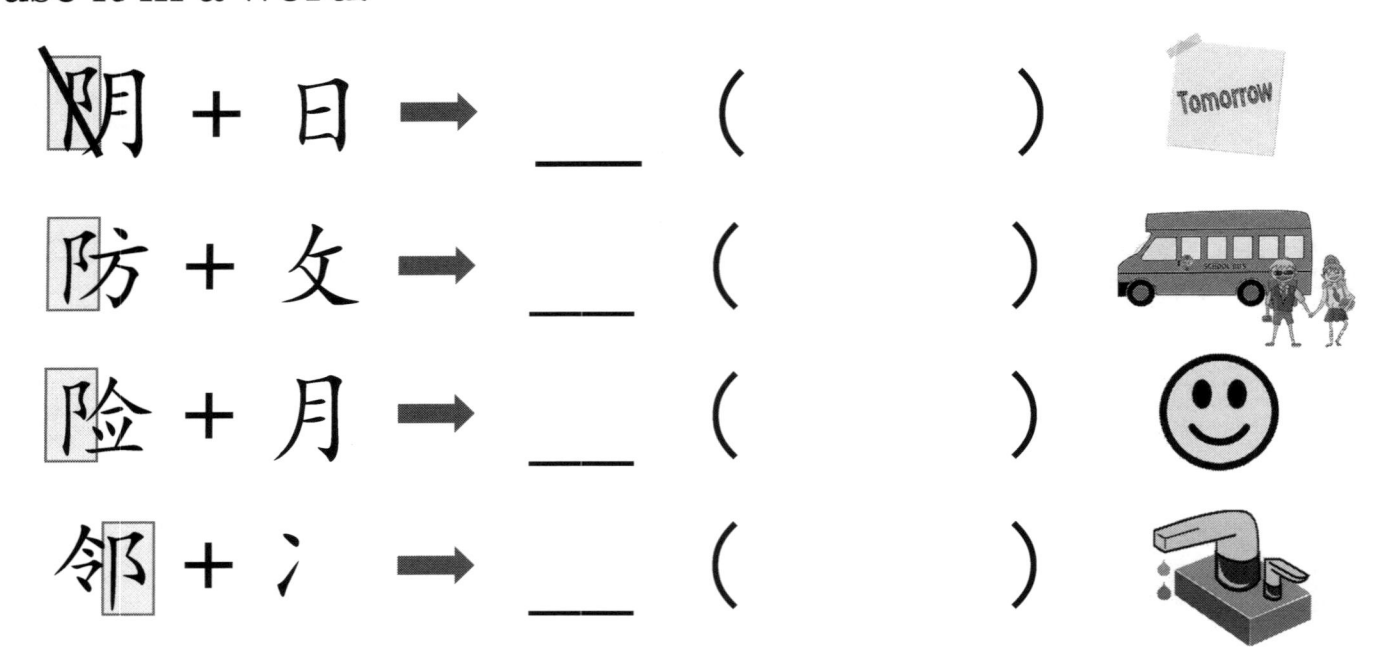

阴 + 日 ➡ ___ (　　　)

防 + 攵 ➡ ___ (　　　)

险 + 月 ➡ ___ (　　　)

邻 + 氵 ➡ ___ (　　　)

Fill in the blanks with characters in the box.

那　邻　院　陌　队

1. 大家排好___，一起做游戏。
　　　　　　　together

2. 我的___居是一个警察。
      jū   jǐng chá

3. 春天，___子里的花都开了。

4. 看，___边有一只红色的小鸟。

5. 不要随便和___生人说话。
      suí biàn

56

部首练习
Semantic Radicals

门字框

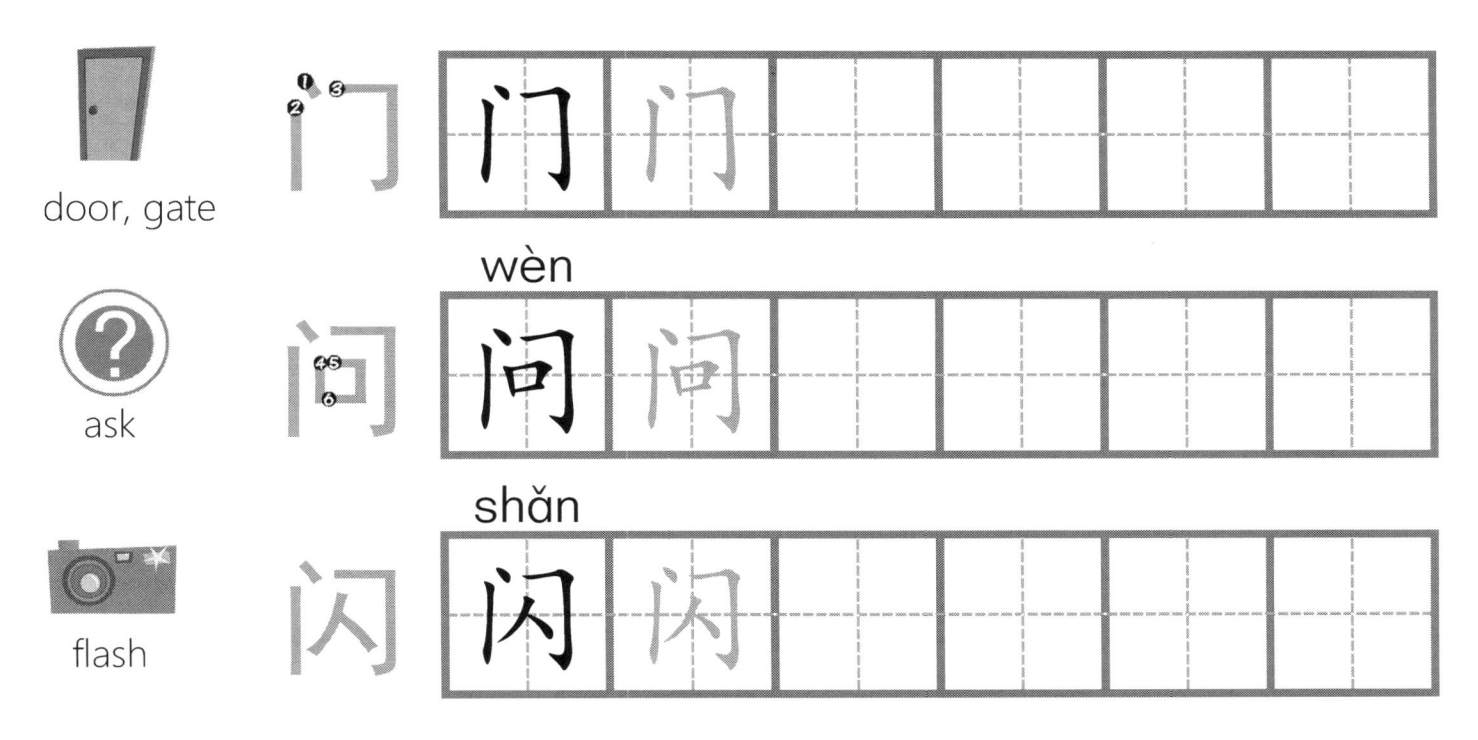

door, gate

门

wèn
问

shǎn
闪

Find and trace 门 in these characters.

请问
may I ask

闪电
lightning

jiān
中间
middle, center

wén
闻花香
smell fragrance

chuǎng
闯红灯
running a red light

mèn
闷热
stuffy and hot

nào
闹钟
alarm clock

nao
热闹
lively

57

Write down the character for each picture.

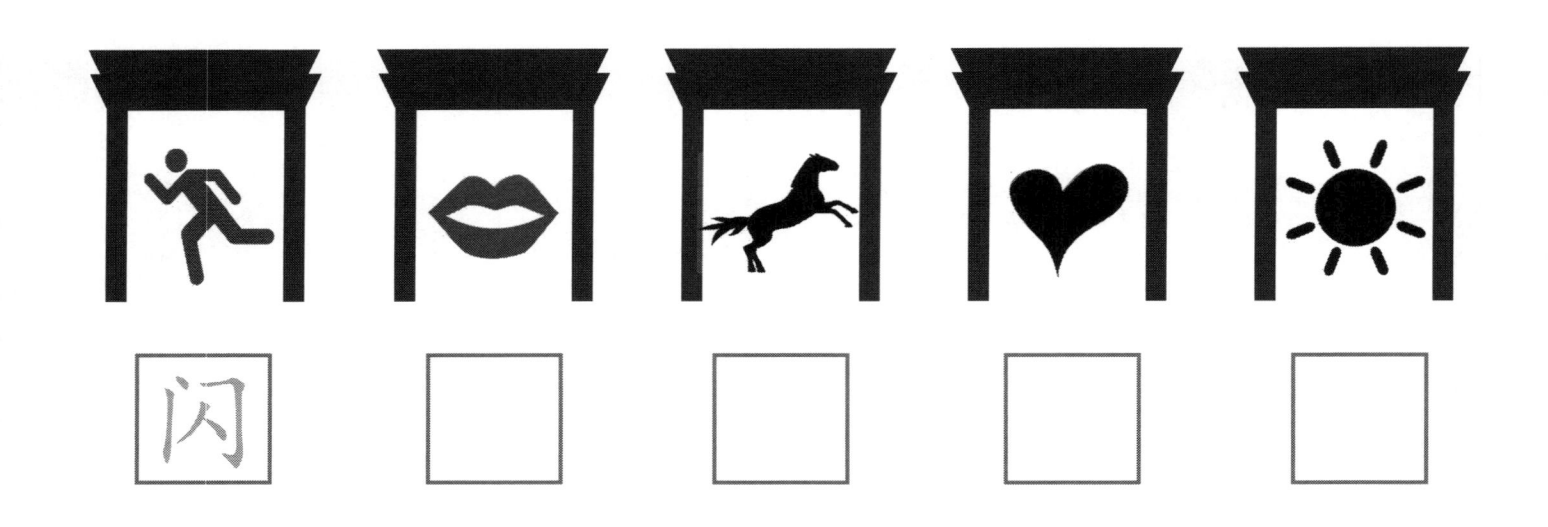

闪 ☐ ☐ ☐ ☐

Ask with 请问 and answer the questions.

1. <u>请问</u>洗手间在哪儿？ <u>洗手间在那边</u>。
   　　restroom

2. ____今天星期几？   今天_____。

3. ____现在几点？   现在_____。

4. ____明天是几月几号？   _____。

5. ____你会说中文吗？   _____。

6. ____你妈妈在家吗？   _____。

7. ____14减9等于几？   _____。

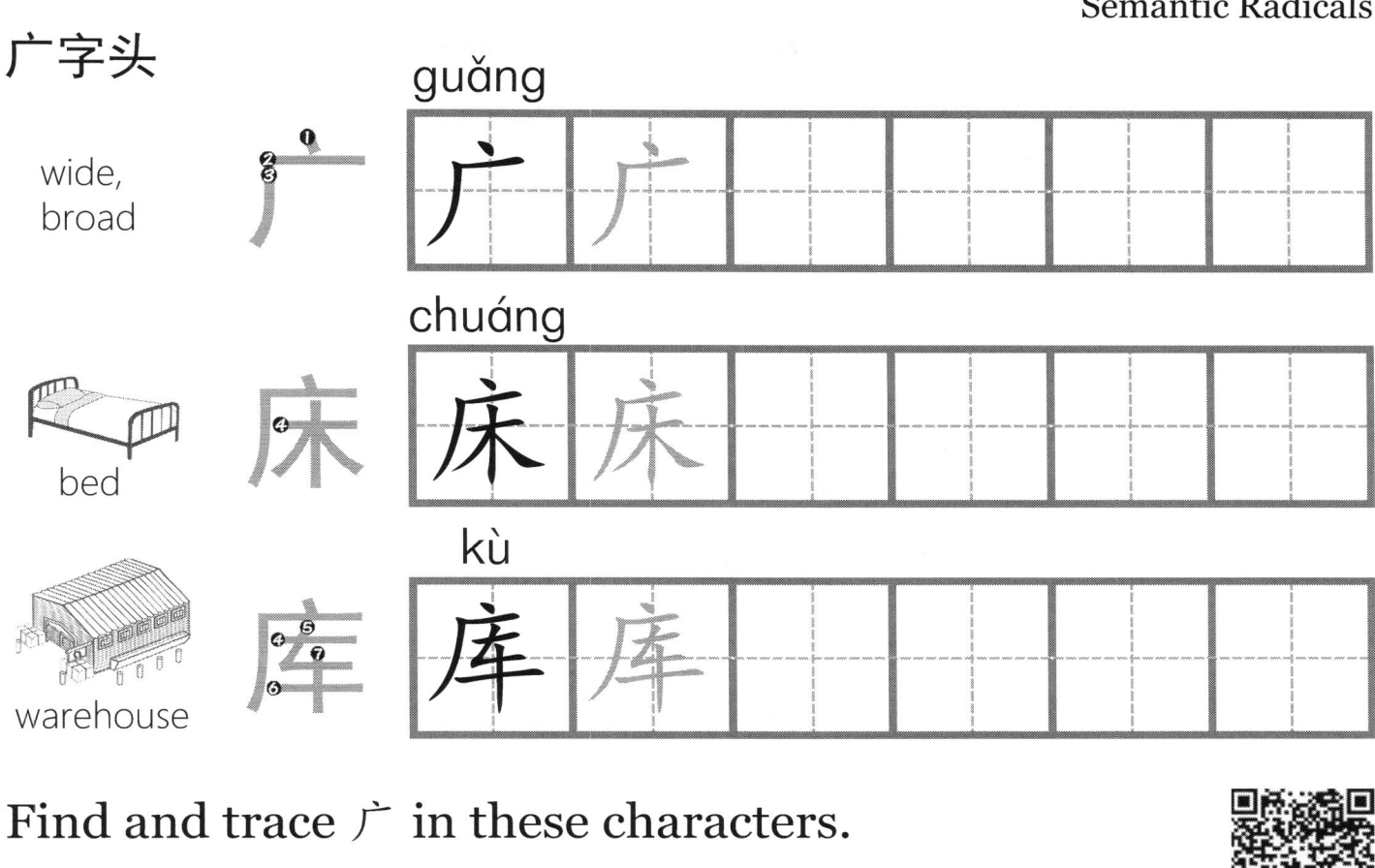

部首练习
Semantic Radicals

广字头

wide, broad

guǎng
广 广

chuáng
床 床

kù
库 库

bed

warehouse

Find and trace 广 in these characters.

chǎng
广场
square, plaza

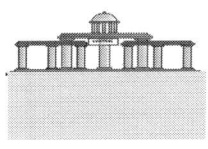

蹦蹦床
trampoline

车库
garage

zuò wèi
座位
seat

dǐ
底下
under

yīng gāi
应该
should

diàn
书店
bookstore

饭店
restaurant

59

Fill in the blanks with characters in the box.

床　库　座　底　店

1. 我每天早上七点起___。

2. 大树___下好凉快。

3. 汽车停在车___里。

4. 昨天我们去饭___吃了中国饭。

5. 请坐在自己的___位上。

Complete the sentences with 应该 or 不应该.

1. 饭前_____洗手。

2. 上学_____迟到。

3. 写作业_____三心二意。

4. 上课说话_____先举手。
   　　　　　　　　xiān jǔ
   　　　　　　　　first raise

5. 牙医说我_____吃太多糖。
   　　　　　　　　　　　　táng

60

部首练习
Semantic Radicals

病字头

sickness radical — 疒 — bìng

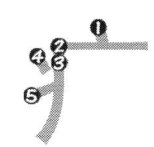

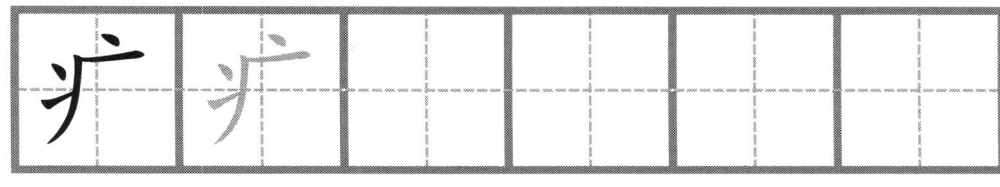

sickness, illness — 病

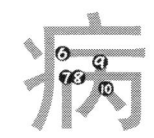

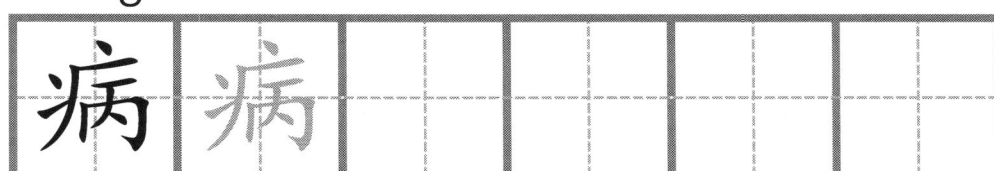

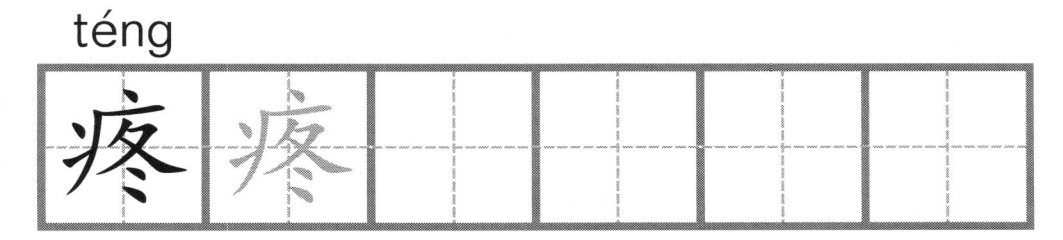

pain, ache — 疼 — téng

Find and trace 疒 in these characters.

生病 — sick

头疼 — headache

zhǐ téng yào
止疼药 — painkillers

药到病除 — The medicine took effect and the symptoms lessoned.

tòng kǔ
痛苦 — suffering

zhuā yǎng
抓痒 — scratch an itch

shòu ruò
瘦弱 — thin and weak

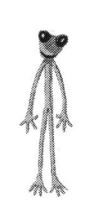

pàng
不胖不瘦 — neither too fat nor too thin

61

Fill in the blanks with characters in the box.

| 病 痒 疼 痛 |

1. 王老师生___了，今天没来上课。

2. 小猴子给老猴子抓___。

3. 别吃太饱，肚子会___的。
   　　　　　　　　　 might

4. 他牙疼不能吃东西，好___苦。

哪里疼？Fill in the blanks. Use the words in the box.

| 头 脚 肚子 牙 |

1. 妹妹吃了太多糖，她____疼。

2. 弟弟吃得太饱，他_____。

3. 妈妈昨晚没睡好觉，她_____。

4. 姐姐穿了一天高跟鞋，她_____。
   　　　　　　　　gēn
   　　　　　　high heels

62

shì
示字旁/示字底　示 ➡ 礻

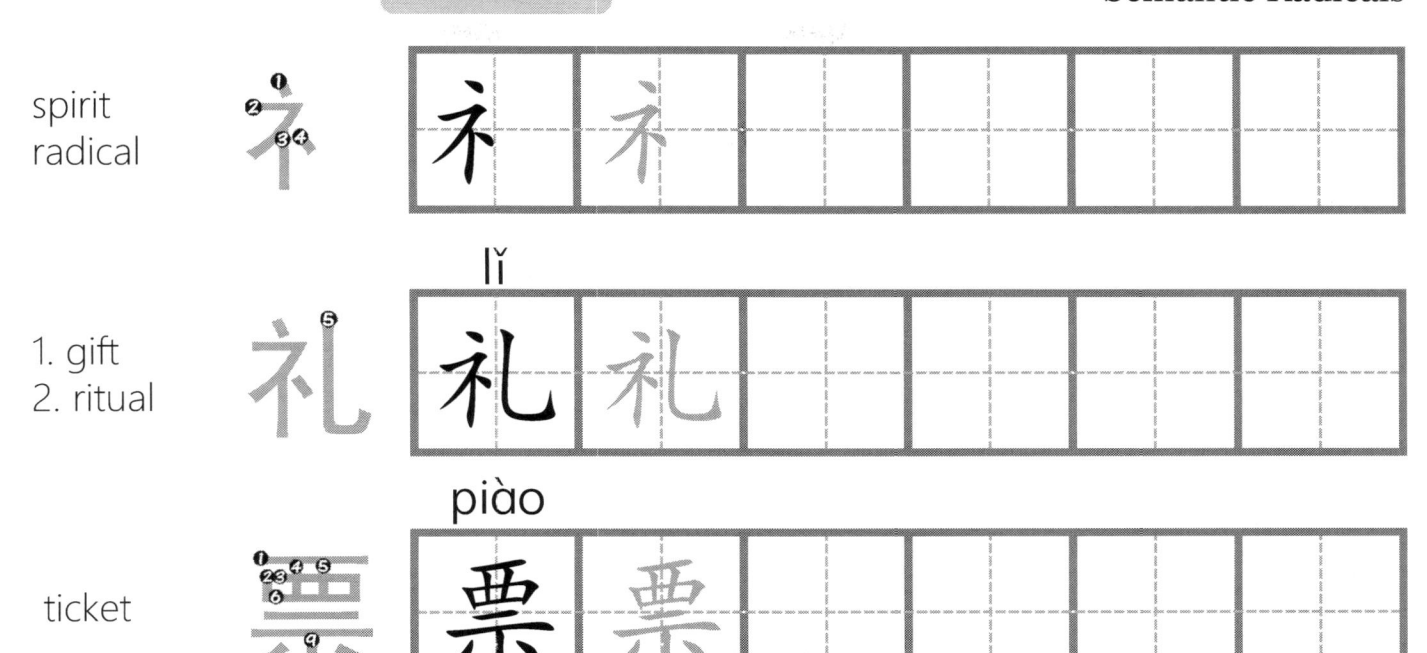

部首练习
Semantic Radicals

spirit radical
礻 礻

lǐ
1. gift
2. ritual
礼 礼

piào
ticket
票 票

Find and trace 礻/示 in these characters.

wù
礼物
gift

shì
电视
TV

飞机票
flight ticket

zǔ
祖父
grandfather

祖母
grandmother

shén
神
God

zhù
祝好
Best Wishes

祝你生日快乐!
Happy Birthday to you!

63

Make words with 票 and fill in the blanks.

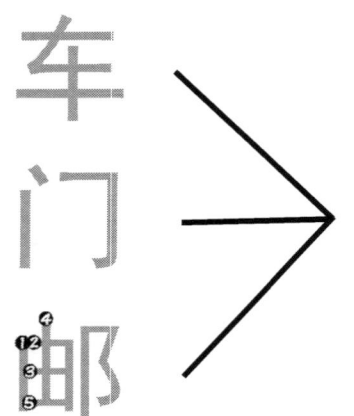

车 ┐
门 ├→ 票 ___
邮 ┘   ___
        ___

1. 坐公交车要买_____。
   (jiāo) (mǎi / buy)

2. 去动物园看动物要买_____。

3. 寄信要买_____。
   (jì xìn / send a letter)

Fill in the blanks with characters in the box.

| 礼 | 神 | 祖 | 祝 |

1. ___你生日快乐！这个___物送给你。

2. 爸爸的父母是我的___父和___母。

3. 我喜欢听___话故事。
   fairy (God) tales

64

部首练习
Semantic Radicals

Now you have learned 22 more radicals! Hooray!

Radical	Variant	Examples	Radical	Variant	Examples
马		骑驮骗	心	忄	您忘怕
火	灬	热黑点	言	讠	说话请
金	钅	钉针钱	彳		行往很
刀	刂	划切剪	辶		过这边
竹	⺮	笔筷篮	攵		收放数
玉	王	球玩琴	口		国圆回
弓		弹弯弟	阝		院那邻
禾		种科秋	门		问闪间
纟		红绿绳	广		床库店
皿		盘盖盆	疒		病疼痒
肉	月	脸脚背	示	礻	票礼祝

65

Quiz Time!

Write the character for each picture. Look at their radicals for hint.

王 月 门 疒 辶 竹

- qiú
- liǎn
- shǎn
- bìng
- guò
- bǐ

广 忄 皿 口 灬 刂

- chuáng
- pà
- pán
- yuán
- rè
- huá

Find the wrong character(s) in each sentence and rewrite them with a correct radical.

1. 哥哥喜欢打⓿球。　　　　　　（ 篮 ）

2. 洛沱不怕热，也不怕渴。（　　）

3. 中国人吃饭用快子。（　　）

4. 西瓜四块线一个。（　　）

5. 住前走五分钟就到了。（　　）

6. 春天冲树，秋天收果。（　　）

7. 今年我上二年圾。（　　）

8. 请座，请喝茶。（　　）

反义词

Opposites

反义词
Opposites

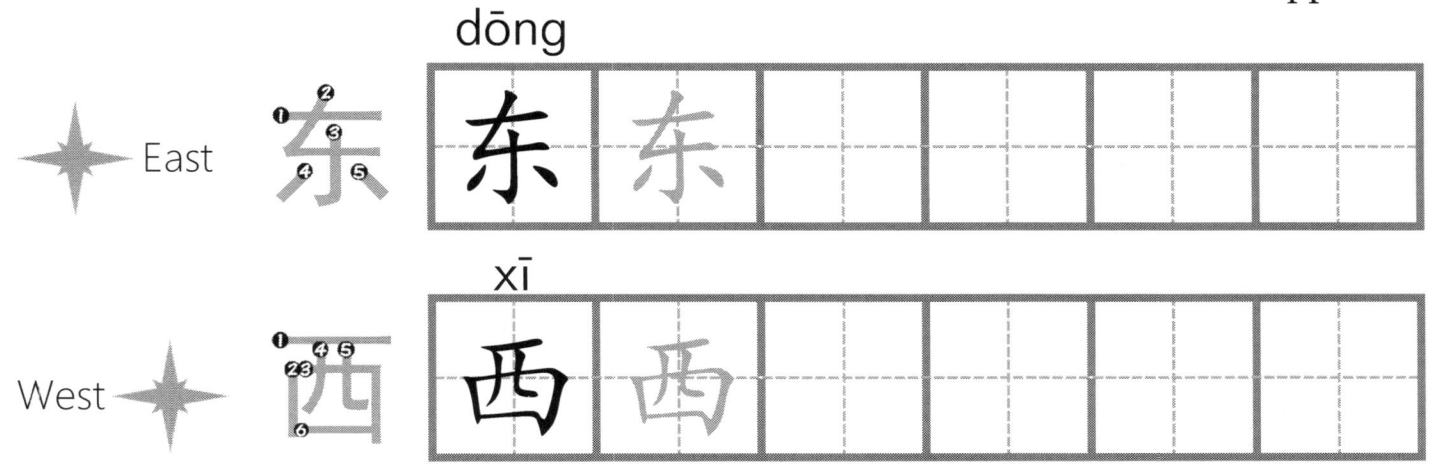

East　dōng　东 东

West　xī　西 西

Fill in the blanks with 东/西.

西 ☀ ☀ 东

1. 早上，太阳从____方升起。
    　　　　　　East　　rise
   晚上，太阳从____方落下。
    　　　　　　West

2. 中国在____方，美国在____方。

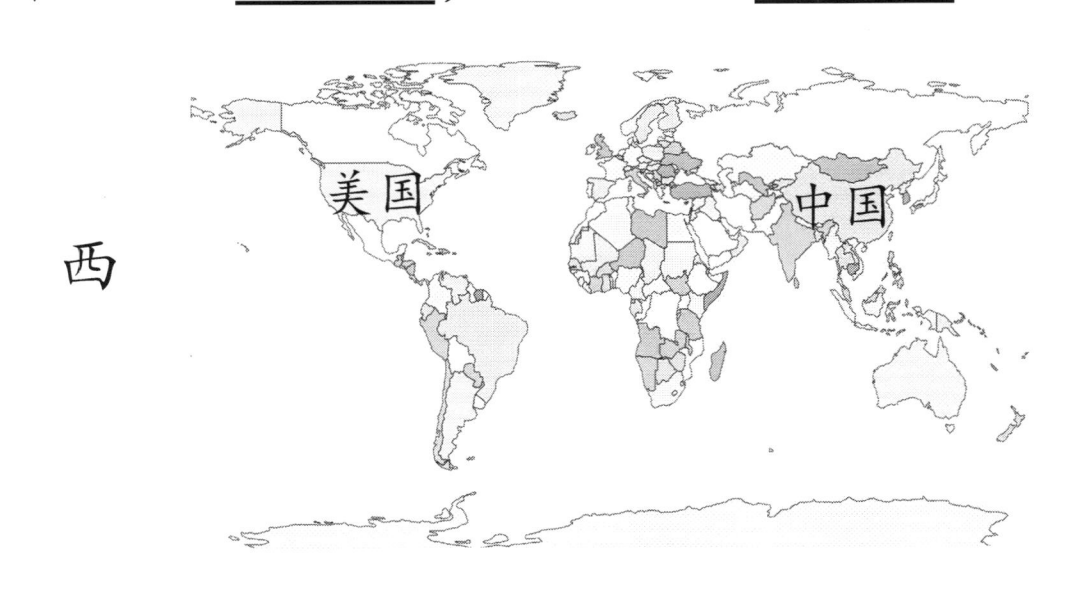

西　　　美国　　　中国　　　东

69

Many things that were introduced to China from the west have 西 in their names. Complete these words with 西.

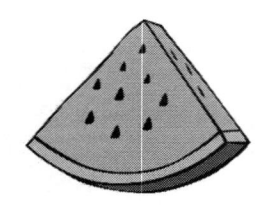

___瓜

shì
___红柿
tomato

lán
___兰花

Some things are from the east, and some things are from the west. That's why "东西" means things. Finish the sentences with 东西.

1. 这是谁的_____？这是我的_____。

dài
2. 明天春游，我要带好多好吃的_____。
　　Spring field trip　　bring

shì jiè　　zuì
3. 世界上最亮的_____是什么？
　world　　brightest

世界上最亮的_____是阳光。

guì
最宝贵的_____是什么？
most precious

最宝贵的_____是时光。
　　　　　　　　time

70

反义词
Opposites

South　nán
南

North　běi
北

Fill in the blanks with 北.

____京
Beijing (Capital city of China)

____美洲

____极熊 生活在____极。
polar bear　live　North Pole

Fill in the blanks with 南.

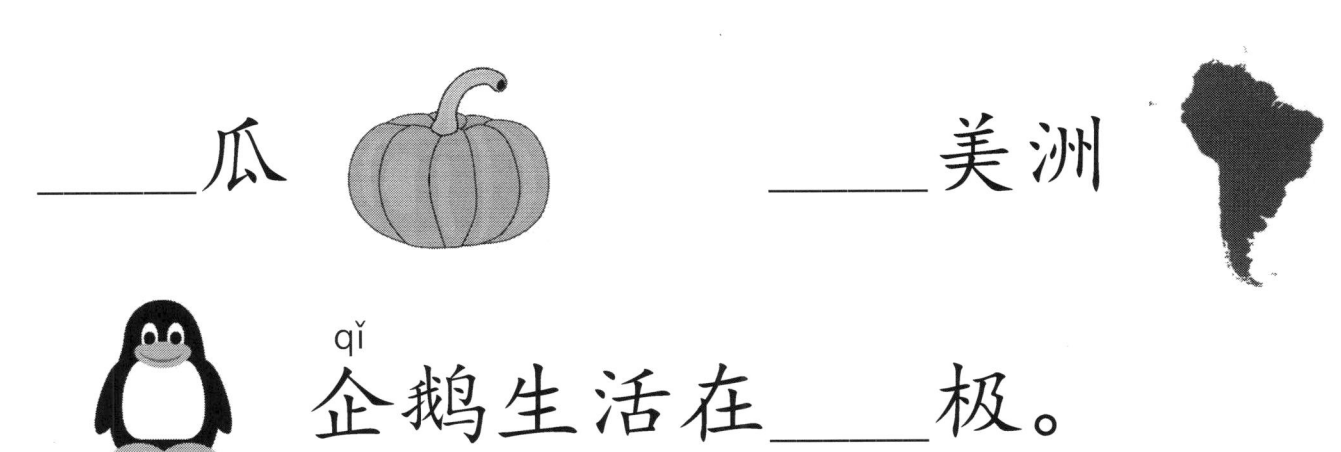

____瓜

____美洲

企鹅生活在____极。
South Pole

71

Fill in the blanks with 东、西、南、北，and the directions between each two, which are 东北、西北、东南、and 西南.

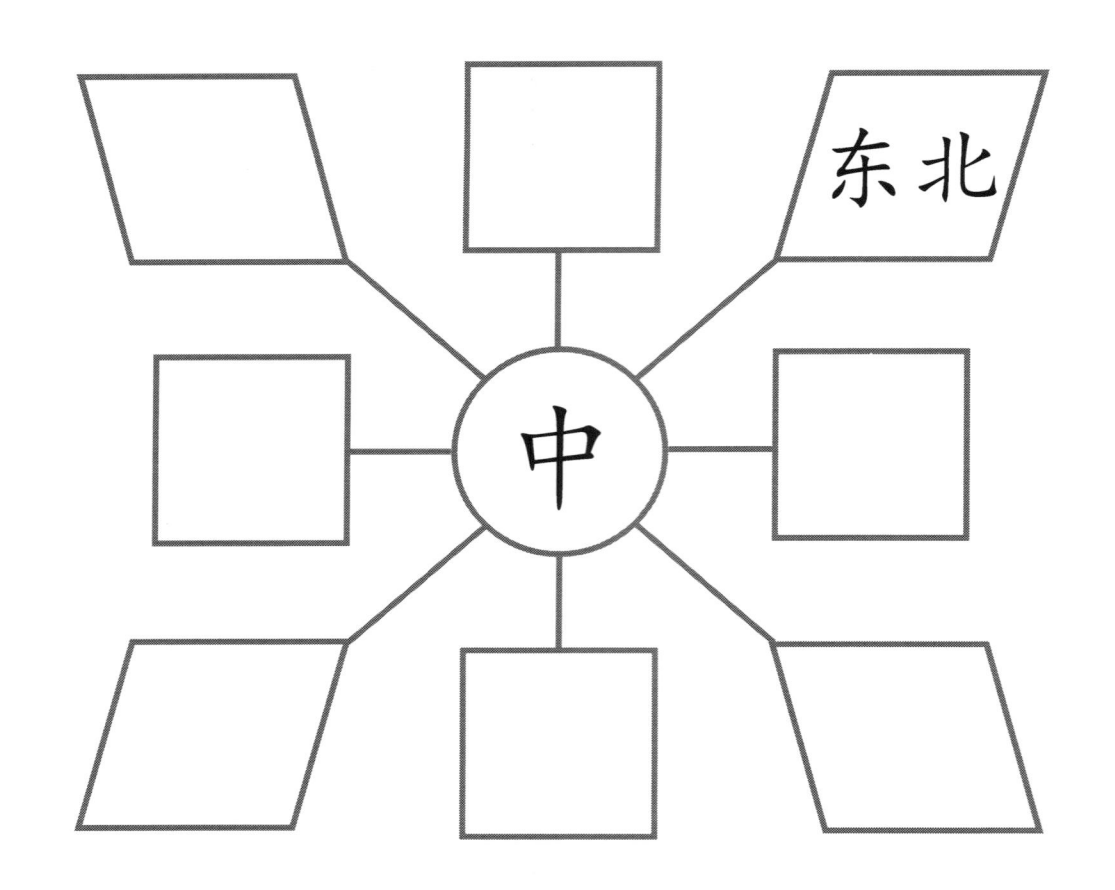

中

东北

North and south hemisphere. Fill in the blanks with 南/北.

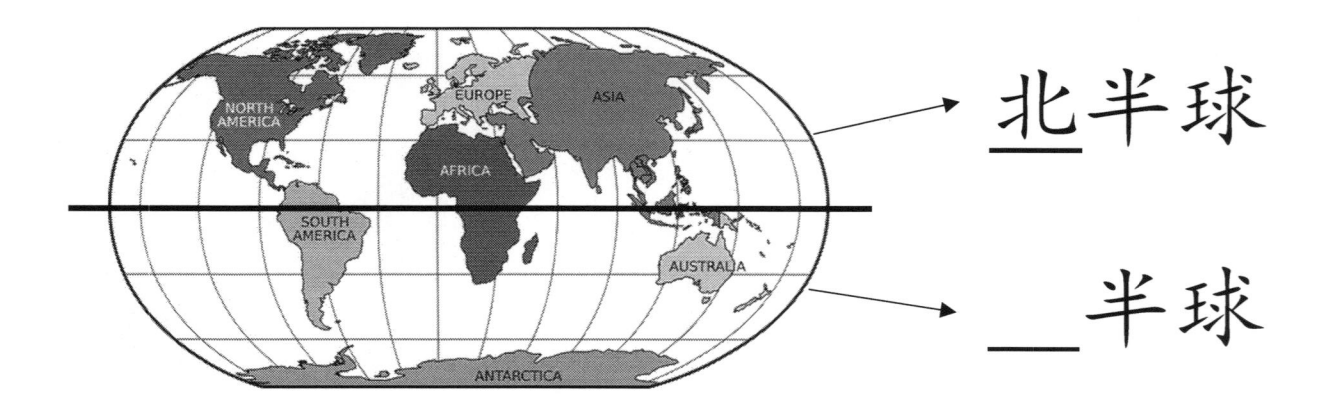

→ __北__半球

→ ___半球

1. 中国和美国都在___半球。
2. 澳大利亚在___半球。
   ào lì yà

72

反义词
Opposites

yuǎn
far 远

jìn
near, close 近

Fill in the blanks with 远/近.

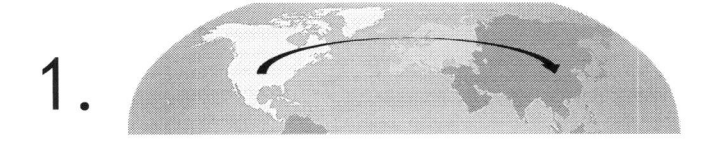

1. 中国离美国＿＿，加拿大离美国＿＿。
   lí
   from

2. 星星离我们＿＿，
   月亮离我们＿＿。

3. 我的学校＿＿，我走路上学。
   姐姐的学校＿＿，她坐校车上学。

73

Read this poem and draw a picture for it.

《画》(by 王维)
huà　　　　　wéi
A painting

远看山有色，
　　　　sè
近听水无声。
　wú shēng
　　　　has no sound
春去花还在，
　　　hái
　　　still
人来鸟不惊。

意思：

远远地看去，山上有鲜亮的颜色。
　　　　　　　　　　　　yán
　　　　　　　　　　　　color
走近了听听，水没有声音。
春天过去了，花儿还在开放。
人走过来，鸟儿也不怕。

Underline the opposites in the poem and write them down.

远 —（　） 　　（　）— 无 　　（　）— 来

74

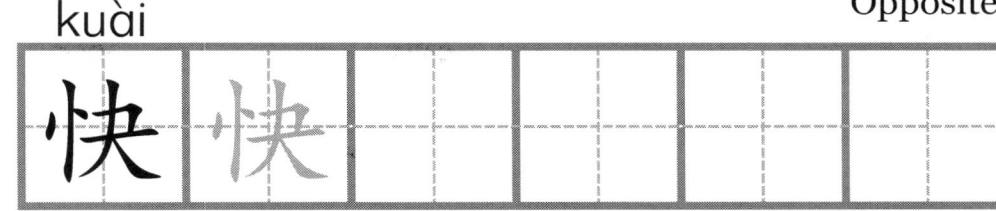

反义词
Opposites

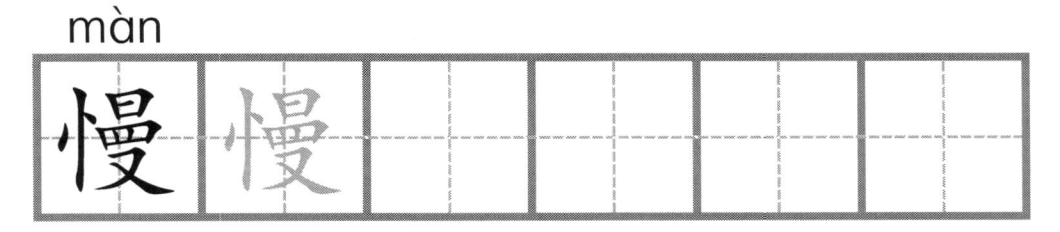

kuài
快

màn
慢

fast, quick
slow

比一比，哪个快？哪个慢？Fill in the blanks with 快/慢.

1.   坐飞机____，
   划船____。

2.   猴子爬树爬得____，
   蜗牛爬树爬得____。

3. 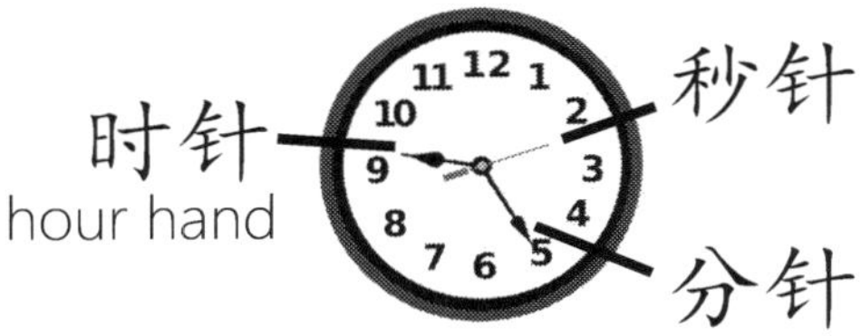 秒针走得____，
   时针走得____。

4.    跑步心跳加 bù ____，
   睡觉心跳减____。

75

Learn these words.

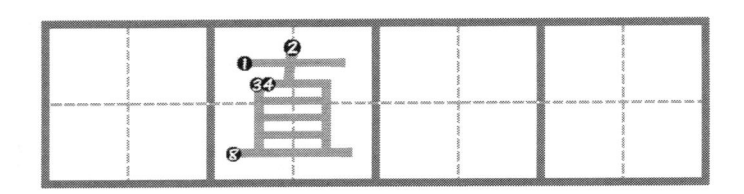

心直口快
zhí

straightforward

意思：心里藏不住话，有话就说。
　　　　　cáng　zhù
　　　　　cannot hide

What is the meaning of 心直口快?

A. 说话快，吃饭也快。

B. 什么话也不说，放在心里。

C. 想到什么就说什么。

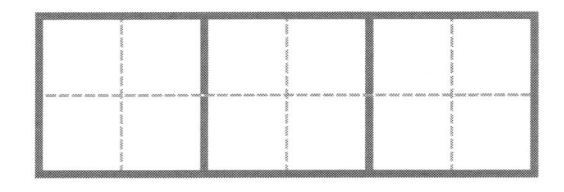

慢吞吞
tūn

意思：做事很慢

Which of the following statements would 慢吞吞 describe?

A. 乌龟走路

B. 猫捉老鼠

C. 哥哥打篮球

76

反义词
Opposites

xīn
新 新 新

new

jiù
旧 旧 旧

old

Fill in the blanks with 新/旧.

1.  ___的一年过去，
   ___的一年到来。

2.  ___的不去，___的不来。
   If the old doesn't go, the new will not come.

3.  ___书包还能用，
   hái néng
   still can be used
   不用买___的。
   mǎi
   no need to buy

4.  认识___朋友，
   不忘老朋友。

77

Learn these words.

喜新厌旧
xǐ ... yàn

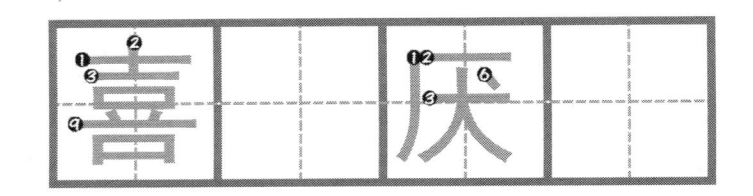

意思：喜欢新的，讨厌旧的。
tǎo — dislike

Which of the following situations would 喜新厌旧 describe?

A. 有了新朋友，还和旧朋友一起玩。

B. 有了新玩具，就不玩旧玩具了。

C. 有一件新衣服，还想要更多新衣服。

耳目一新

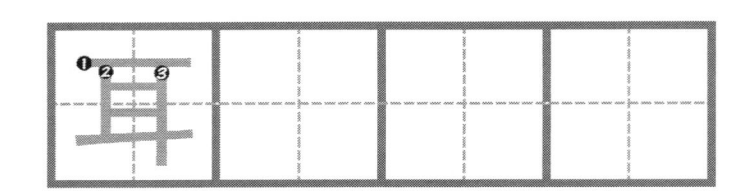

意思：听到和看到的跟以前不同，感觉很新鲜。
yǐ — tóng — gǎn jué

What you hear and see are very different from before, and that makes you feel very fresh.

Which of the following situations would 耳目一新 describe?

A. 妈妈几天没休息好，感觉_____。
  a few

B. 我几个月没吃过饺子了，感觉_____。

C. 爸爸几年没去中国了，一下飞机感觉_____。

78

反义词
Opposites

duì
对

cuò
错

Read the sentences and write 对 or 错 in the boxes.

1. 饭前要洗手。

2. 垃圾丢在桌子上。

3. 上课说话要先举手。
   xiān jǔ

4. 红灯行，绿灯停。

5. 太阳从西边升起。

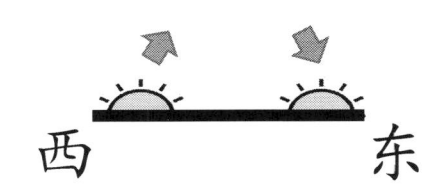

西　　东

Learn this word.

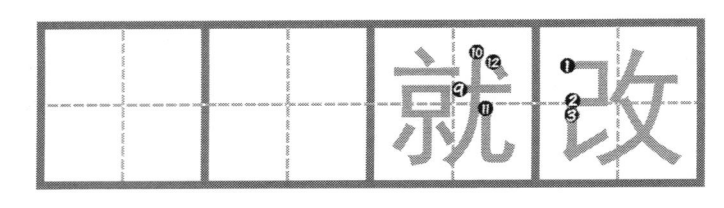

zhī cuò jiù gǎi
知错就改
then correct it

意思：知道自己错了就马上改正。

Which of the following stories describes 知错就改?

A.

一只乌鸦(wū yā / crow)口渴了，就去找水喝。它看到一个瓶(píng / bottle)子，里面有一些水。可是水太少，怎么喝到呢？乌鸦想了想，找来一些小石子放到瓶子里。很快，水面升高了，乌鸦就喝到水了。

B.

小猫去钓鱼，一会儿捉蜻蜓，一会儿捉蝴蝶，一条鱼也没钓到。妈妈说，钓鱼要一心一意，不能三心二意。后来，小猫听了妈妈的话，钓上来一条大鱼。

反义词
Opposites

zhēn
true, real 真

jiǎ
false, fake 假

True or False? Write 真的/假的 in the parenthesis.

1. 袋鼠的个子矮，生活(huó)在中国。（　　）

2. 长颈鹿的个子高，爱吃树叶。（　　）

3. 大熊猫爱吃鱼，生活在北极。（　　）

4. 骆驼喜欢下雨，生活在海边。（　　）

5. 鲸(jīng)是地球上最大的动物。（　　）
whale

81

真的 also means really. Ask questions with 真的.

1. 圣诞老人_____会送给我礼物吗？

2. 牙仙女_____会拿走我的牙齿吗？

3. 你_____会拉手风琴吗？

4. 纸_____是用树做的吗？

真+**Adjective** is often used for exclamations. Change these statements into exclamatory sentences with 真.

今天很热。 ⟶ 今天真热！

1. 这个西瓜很甜。_____

2. 这条围巾很漂亮。_____

3. 今天的作业很多。_____

4. 姐姐弹琴很好听。_____

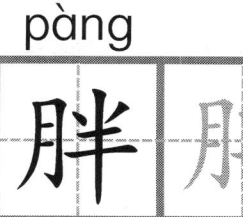

反义词
Opposites

pàng
chubby, fat 胖 胖 胖

shòu
thin, skinny 瘦 瘦 瘦

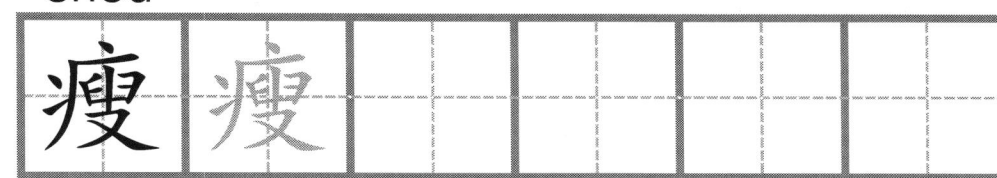

Fill in the blanks with 胖/瘦.

zhǎng
1. 熊猫长得___, 猴子长得___。

2. 宝宝的脸___, 姐姐的脸___。

3. 弟弟的脚___, 哥哥的脚___。

4. ___人怕热, ___人怕冷。

83

Look at the pictures below and fill in the blanks with these opposites.

长 短 高 矮 胖 瘦 黑 白

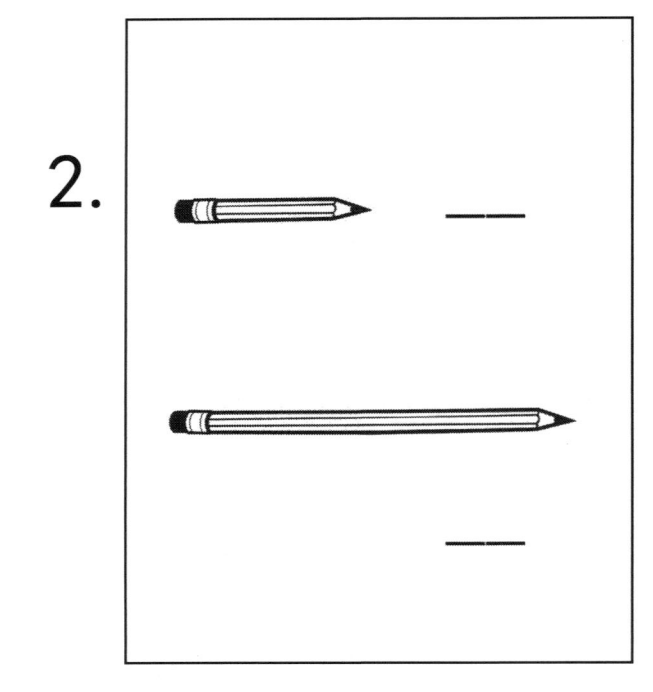

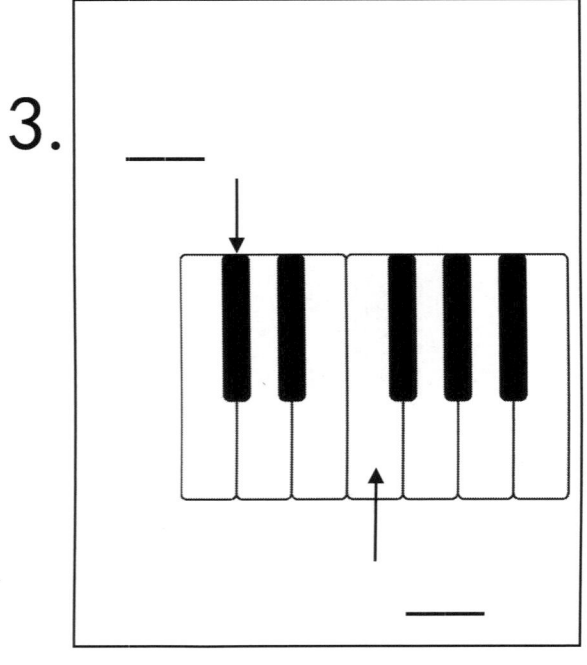

1. 高 ___

2. ___ / ___

3. ___ / ___

4. ___ / ___

84

反义词
Opposites

qīng
light 轻 轻

zhòng
heavy 重 重

Fill in the blanks with 轻/重.

1. 羽毛___,   石头___。
   yǔ
   feather

2. 树叶___,   树干___。
                 gàn
                 trunk, log

3. 小兔子走路___, 大象走路___。

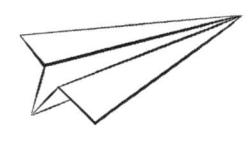

4. 一张纸___,   一本书___。
                 běn
                 a   book

85

哪个轻，哪个重？

Look at the scales and complete the sentences with 轻/重.

1. 两个苹果___，
三个橙子___。
两个苹果比三个橙子___，
三个橙子比两个苹果___。

2. 熊猫___，鸭子___。
熊猫比鸭子___，
鸭子比熊猫___。

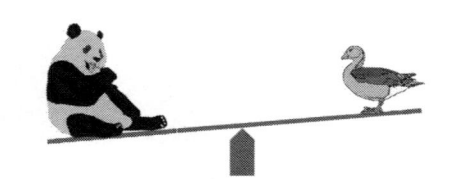

3. 羽毛球___，篮球___。
badminton

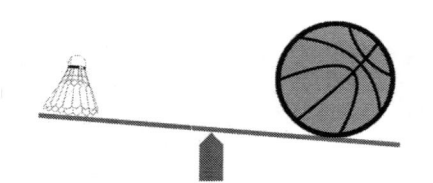

_____，
_____。

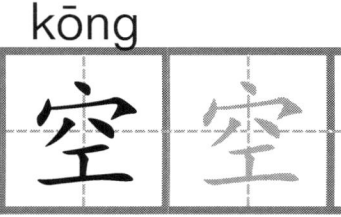

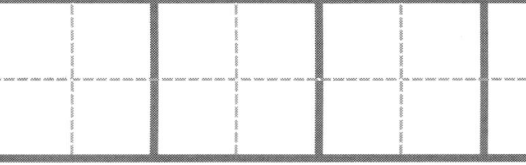

反义词
Opposites

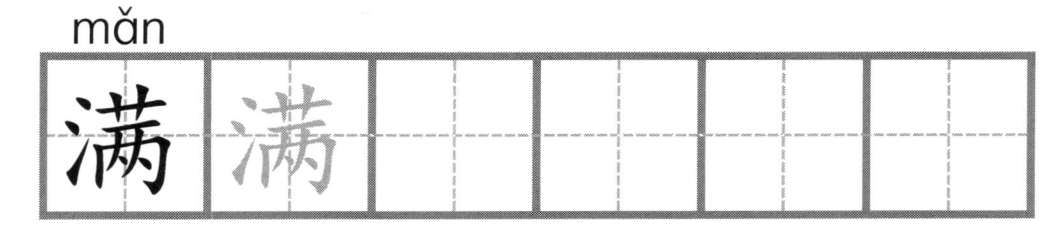

kōng 空 — empty

mǎn 满 — full

Fill in the blanks with 空/满.

1.  这个杯子___，那个杯子___。

2. 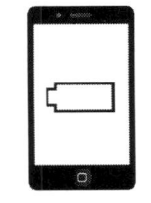 电池(chí, battery)___了，手机没电了。 电池___了，手机有电了。

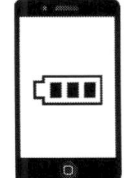

3.  冰箱___了，要买菜了。 买菜回来，冰箱___了。

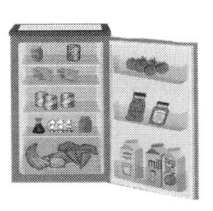

87

Fill in the boxes by the code. Then read the poem and draw a picture for it.

《山居秋暝》 An Autumn Evening in the Mountains (by 王维)

1. 山	2. 雨	3.
天气	4. 来	5.
明月	sōng 松	间照
qīng 清	quán 泉	6. 石	liú 流

，
。
，
。

1. "满"的反义词
2. "旧"的反义词
3. "前"的反义词
4. "早"的反义词
5. 夏天过后的季节
6. "下"的反义词

意思：空空的山里刚(gāng/just)下了雨，到了晚上，秋意正凉。明亮的月光从松(sōng)树间(pine)照下来，清清的泉(quán/spring)水从石头上流(liú/flow)过。

88

反义词
Opposites

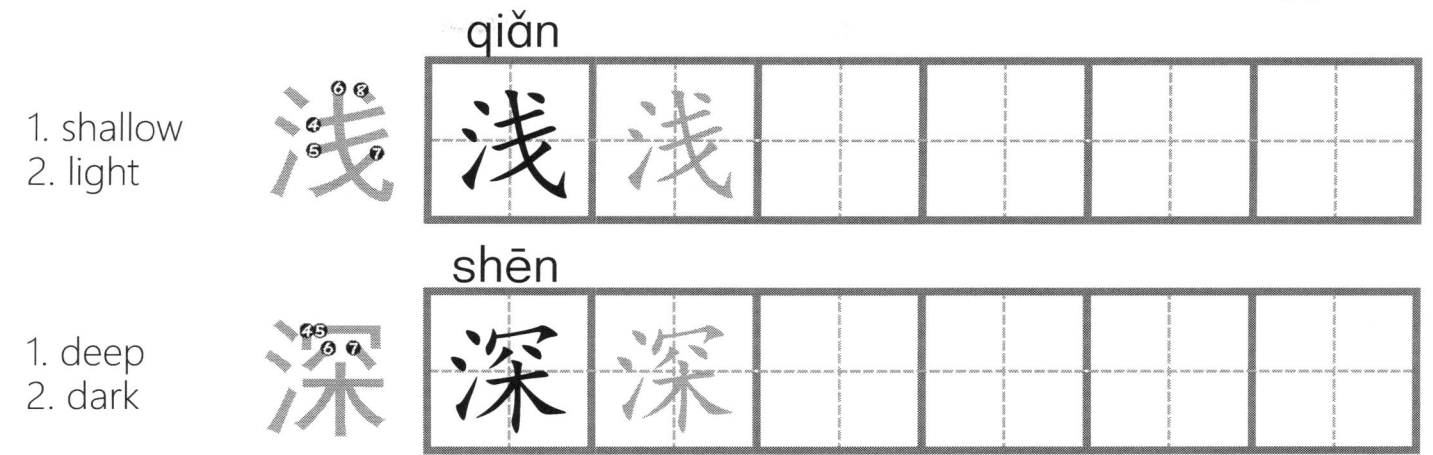

1. shallow
2. light
浅 qiǎn

1. deep
2. dark
深 shēn

Fill in the blanks with 浅/深.

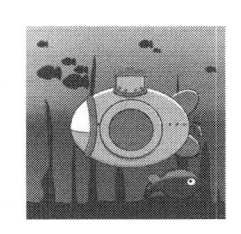

1. 小溪的水＿＿＿，
大海的水＿＿＿。

2. 游泳池的一边＿＿＿，
一边＿＿＿。

3. 春天，树叶的颜色＿＿＿，
夏天，树叶的颜色＿＿＿。

89

深色和浅色

Color the crayons with dark and light colors.

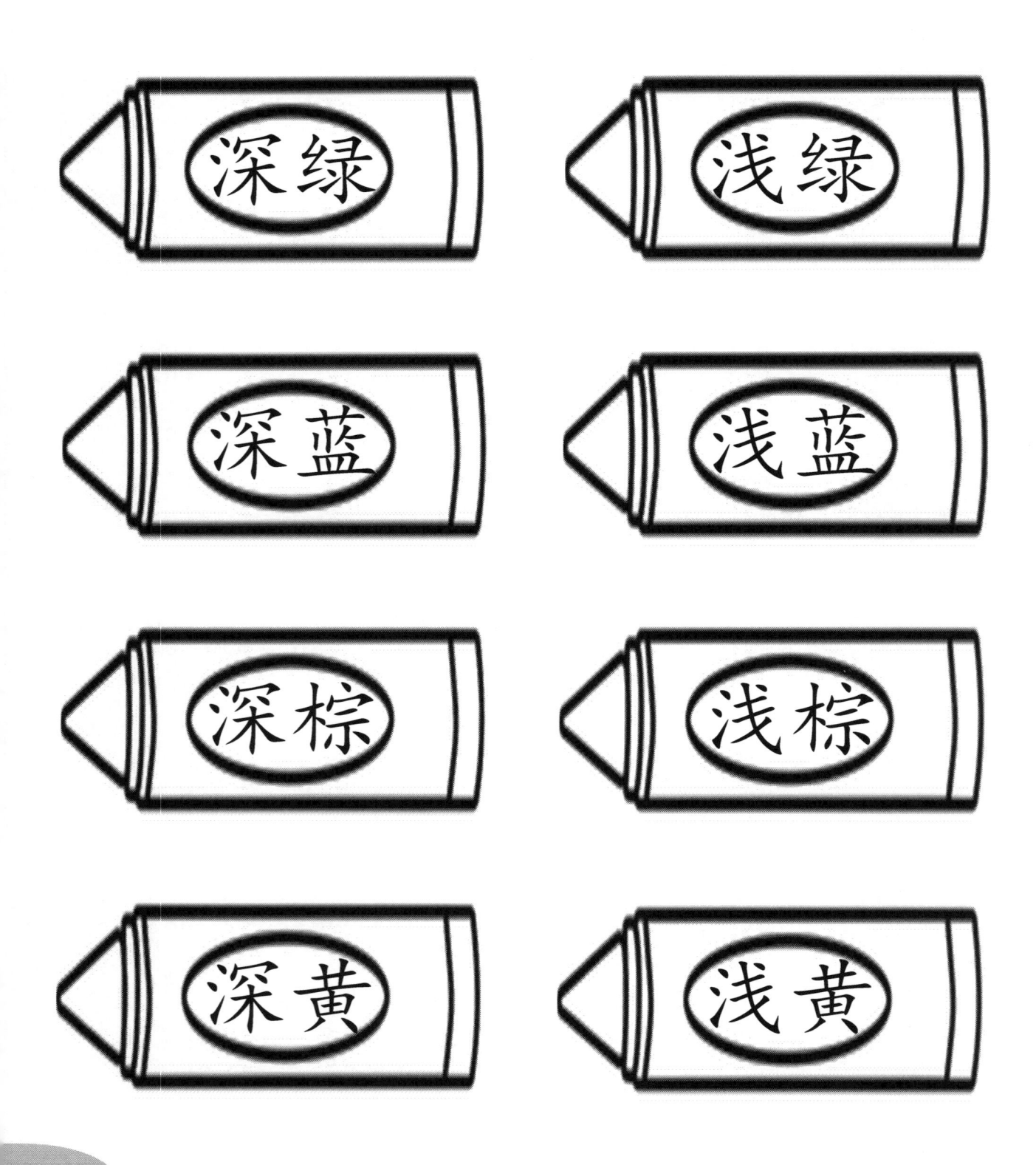

深绿	浅绿
深蓝	浅蓝
深棕	浅棕
深黄	浅黄

反义词
Opposites

float　fú 浮

sink　chén 沉

什么浮在水上？什么沉在水底？
Fill in the blanks with 浮/沉.

1. 小船___在水上，
鱼钩(gōu)___在水底。
hook

2. 羽毛___在水上，
石头___在水底。

3. 救生圈(quān)___在水上，
life buoy
潜水环(qián huán)___在水底。
diving ring

91

浮沉实验 (shí yàn) Float or Sink Experiment

You'll need:

一盆水　　一分钱　　一块橡皮
一个苹果　一片树叶(piàn)　一把钥匙

You'll find out:

什么东西浮在水上？
什么东西沉在水底？

Draw and record your result.

1. 一分钱＿＿在＿＿＿＿。

2. 橡皮＿＿＿＿＿＿＿。

3. 钥匙＿＿＿＿＿＿＿。

4. ＿＿＿＿＿＿＿＿＿。

5. ＿＿＿＿＿＿＿＿＿。

反义词
Opposites

cū
1. thick
2. rough
粗 粗

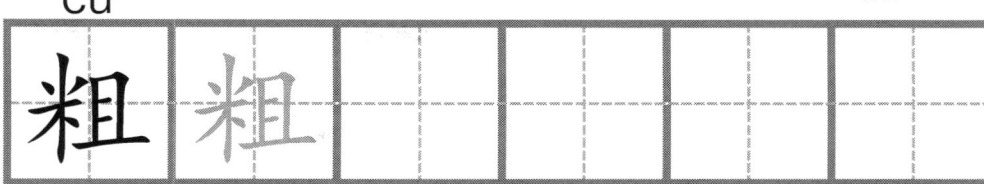

xì
1. thin
2. fine
细 细

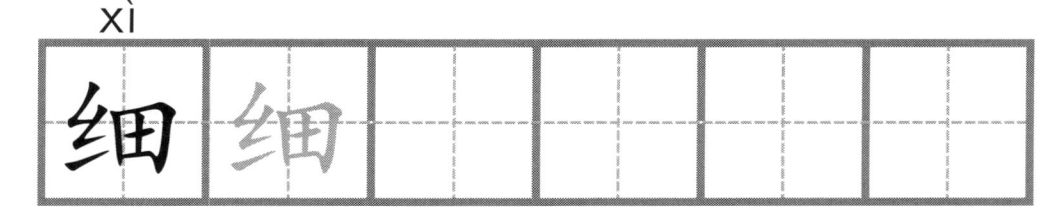

Fill in the blanks with 粗/细.

1.   松鼠的尾巴＿＿＿，
   猴子的尾巴＿＿＿。

2.   男人的声音＿＿＿，
   女人的声音＿＿＿。

3.   爸爸的眉(méi)毛＿＿＿，
   我的眉毛＿＿＿。

4. 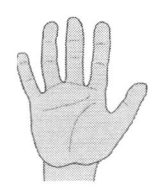 大拇(mǔ)指(zhǐ)＿＿＿，
   (thumb)
   小拇指＿＿＿。

93

Learn these words.

粗心大意

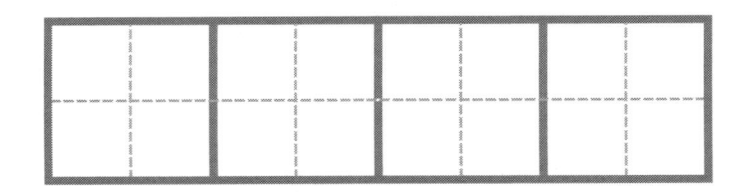

意思：做事马虎，不细心。
　　　　　careless　not careful

Which of the following statements describes 粗心大意?

A. 小鸡怕水，不敢游泳。

B. 冬天要来了，北方的小鸟都往南方飞。

C. 弟弟写字老是这里少一笔，那里多一笔。
　　　　　　　often

胆大心细

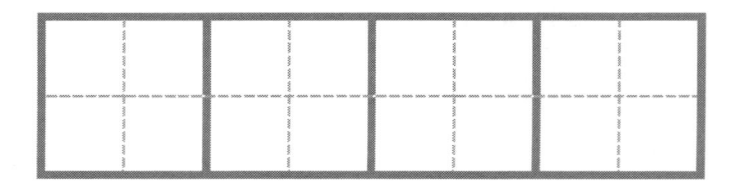

意思：胆子大，心眼儿细。
　　　　brave　　　careful

What does 胆大心细 mean?

A. 又漂亮又细心

B. 又勇敢又细心

C. 又勇敢又漂亮

94

反义词
Opposites

wide   kuān
宽 宽 宽

narrow   zhǎi
窄 窄 窄

Fill in the blanks with 宽/窄.

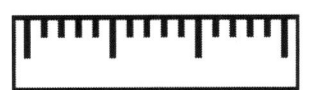

1. 这把尺子___， 那把尺子___。
   chǐ
   this ruler

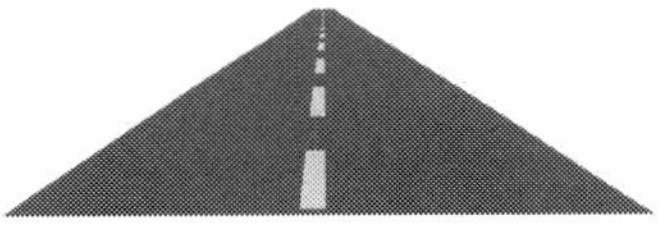

2. 这条马路___， 那条小道___。
                    trail, path

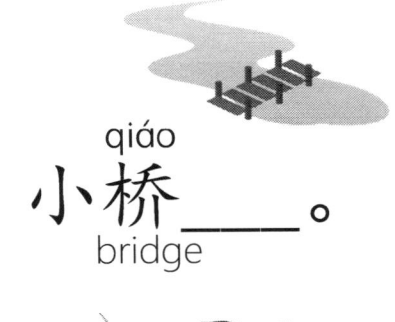

3. 河水___， 小桥___。
                qiáo
                bridge

4. 衣服___， 袖子___。
                xiù

95

Learn this word.

放宽心

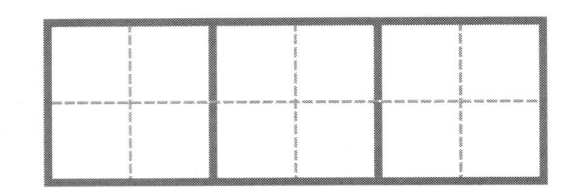

意思：放松，不用担^{dān}心。 Relax and don't worry.

In which of the following situations would you use 放宽心?

A. 我和爸爸一起过马路。我说："爸爸，我会看红绿灯了，您_____吧。"

B. 在学校，我问老师："这个字我不认识，请您_____。"

C. 我和好朋友一起做游戏。我不小心踩^{cǎi}到了他的脚，我说："对不起，_____。"
   step on

Say this tongue twister.   扁担^{biǎndan}和板凳^{bǎndèng}
A Carrying Pole and a Bench

扁担长，板凳宽，

扁担放在板凳上。

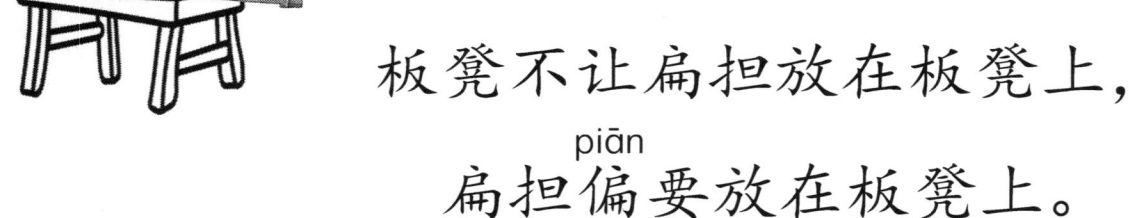

板凳不让扁担放在板凳上，

扁担偏^{piān}要放在板凳上。
         determined

Fun Time!

Match the opposites. Cut and paste.

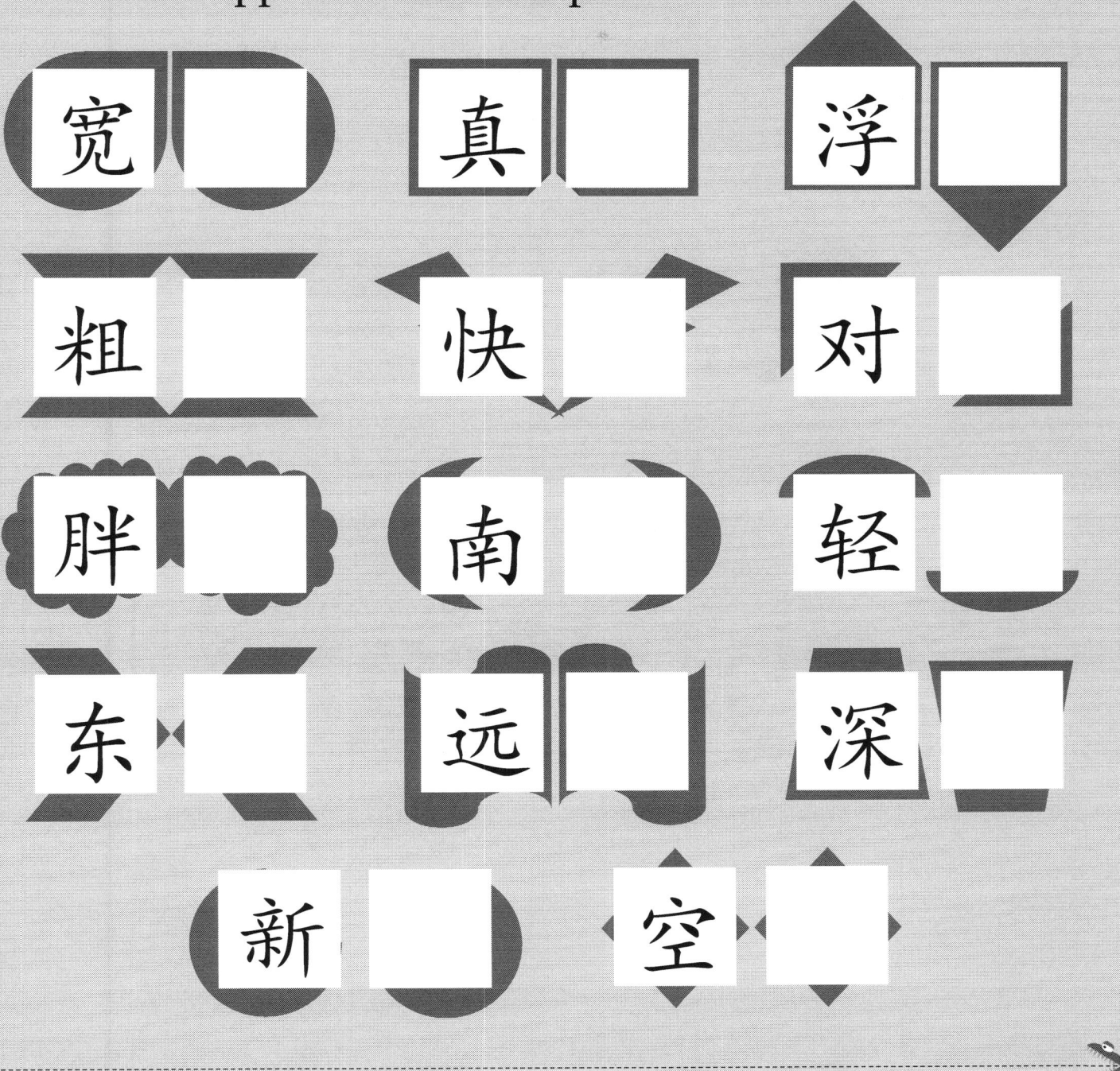

宽 ☐	真 ☐	浮 ☐
粗 ☐	快 ☐	对 ☐
胖 ☐	南 ☐	轻 ☐
东 ☐	远 ☐	深 ☐
	新 ☐	空 ☐

| 窄 | 细 | 重 | 满 | 错 | 沉 | 假 |
| 西 | 北 | 瘦 | 慢 | 近 | 旧 | 浅 |

最常用字

Sight Words

最常用字
Sight Words

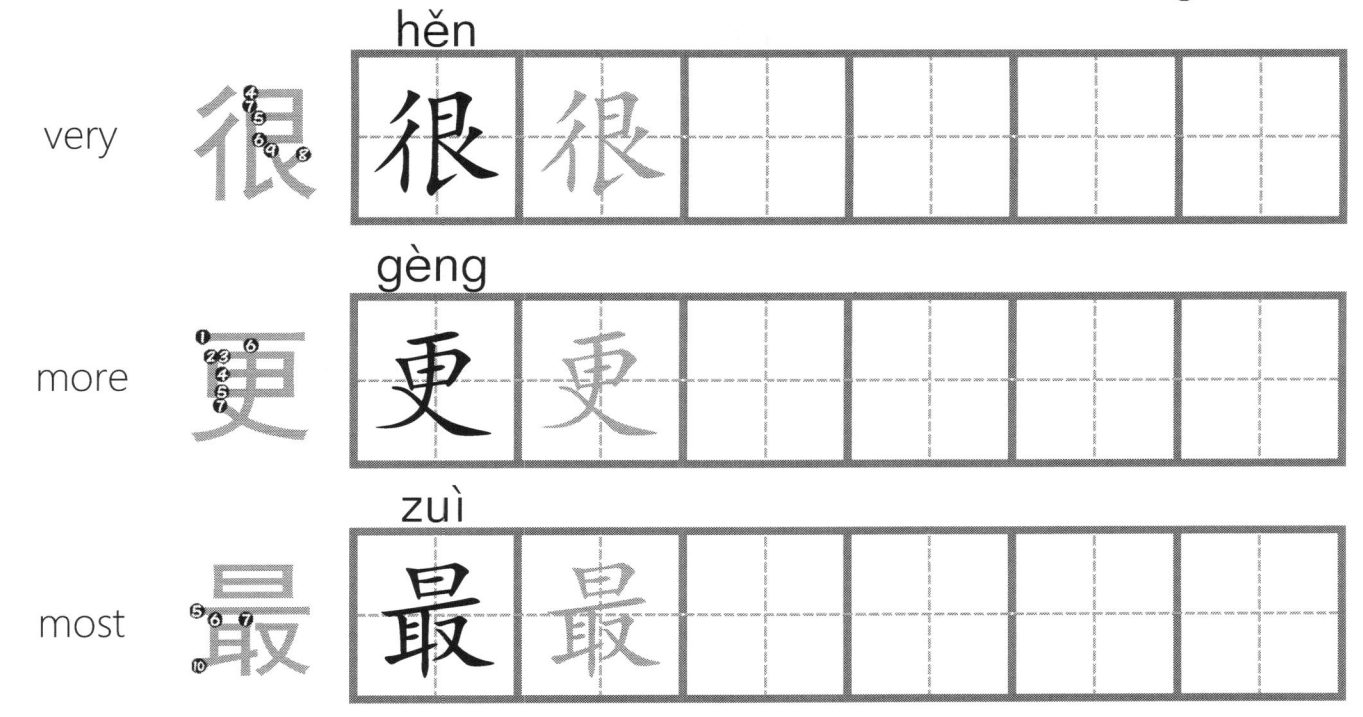

very 很 hěn

more 更 gèng

most 最 zuì

Look and write with 很，更，and 最.

很多 ___ ___   ___ ___

老虎___大，大象___大，鲸___大。
whale / jīng

Make sentences with 很，更，最.

汽车很快，火车_____，飞机_____。

马很高， 骆驼_____， 长颈鹿(jǐng lù)_____。

Draw and write your own 很，更，最 sentences.

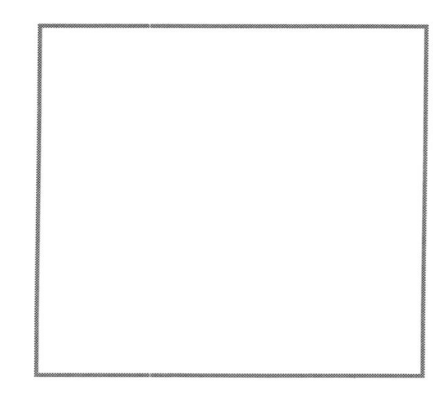

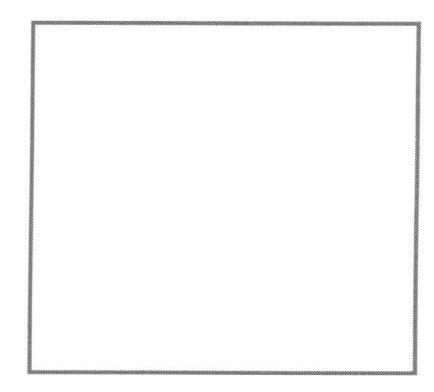

_____，_____，_____。

最常用字
Sight Words

1. highest, senior,
2. too, overly

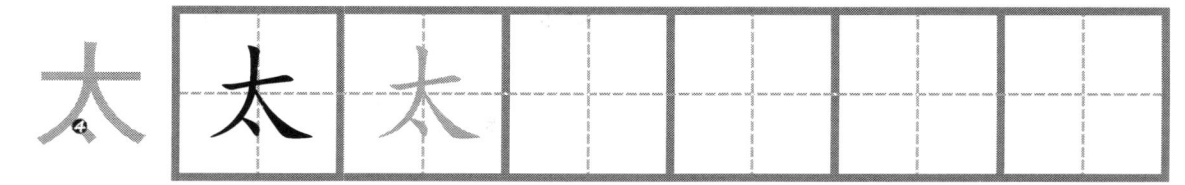

太 太 太

太 is often used with 了 to express excessiveness. ("too much")
Complete the words with 太…了.

<u>太</u>重<u>了</u>　　__慢__　　__脏__(zāng)　　__胆小__

Make sentences with 太…（了）. Use the words in the parenthesis.

1. 山_____，我不敢往下看。　　（高）
   (too high)

2. 蛋糕_____，不要吃多。　　（甜）

3. 这_____，我不相信。　　（奇怪）
   (xiāng xìn / believe)

4. 爸爸_____，没时间和我玩。（忙）

5. 走路_____，我们骑车好吗？（慢）

101

太…了 is also used for exclamation, meaning "So…!" Use 太…了 with these words to complete the sentences.

可爱　可怕　好　美

1. 小猫_____，我真想要一只。

2. 这里_____，我们都不想回家了。

3. _____！明天就放假了！
   （jià holiday, break）

4. 院子里有一条蛇！_____！

不太 means "not very". Complete the sentences with 不太…. Use words in the parenthesis.

1. 那个公园_____。（大）

2. 我中午吃得多，现在还_____。（饿）
   （xiàn now）

3. 我有点儿累了，_____出去。（想）
   （lèi）

4. 妈妈今天_____。（高兴）

5. 这么做_____。（好）
   like this

102

最常用字
Sight Words

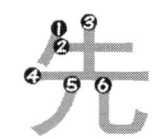

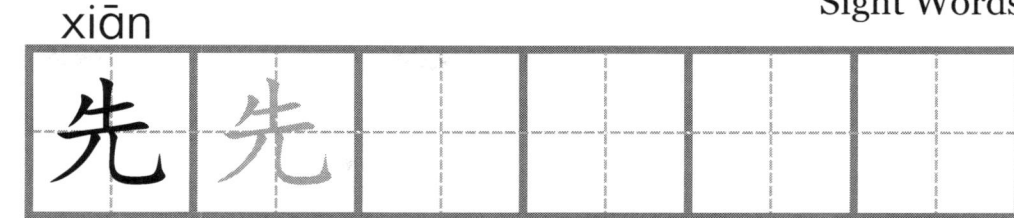

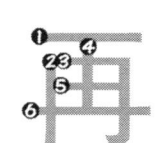

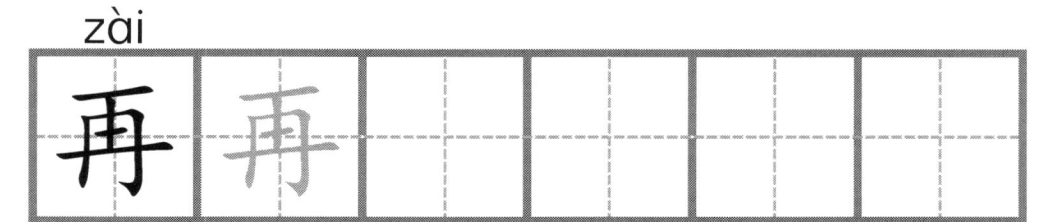

xiān
1. former,
2. first
先

zài
1. again,
2. then
再

Complete the words with 先.

___生
Sir, Mr.

祖___
ancestor

bèn
笨鸟___飞
clumsy birds have to start flying early

Complete the words with 再.

___见

huān yíng   cì
欢迎你下次___来
welcome   next time

biàn
请你___说一遍
say it once again

让我___想一想

103

Fill in the blanks with 先 or 再.

1. 我不太饿，你___吃吧。

2. 我妈妈还没来，你___回家吧。

3. 我___走了，下次___见！

4. 欢迎你下次___来我家玩！

Make sentences with 先 and 再.

1. ___买票，___上车。

2. ___脱鞋子，_____。
   (tuō xié / take off)

3. ___做完作业，_____。

4. ___穿衣服，_____。

5. ___洗手，_____。

6. ___吃饱肚子，_____。

104

最常用字
Sight Words

shí
时

时候
time, moment

hòu
候

…的时候 is used to express "when…".
Complete the sentences with …的时候.

1. 上课＿＿＿＿＿＿，说话要先举(jǔ)手。

2. 走路＿＿＿＿＿＿，请不要玩手机。

3. 妹妹哭＿＿＿＿＿＿，请你抱(bào)抱她。
   hug

4. 爷爷小＿＿＿＿＿＿，也爱玩沙子。

5. 爸爸上大学＿＿＿＿＿＿，认识了妈妈。

6. 妈妈不在家＿＿＿＿＿＿，我和爸爸一起做饭。

105

妈妈不在家的时候

What would happen when your mommy is not home? Draw and write. Some of the characters may include 我，爸爸，哥哥，姐姐，弟弟，妹妹，小狗, etc.

_____

_____

_____

_____

什么时候 is used to ask about "when" in questions. Ask about the underlined words with 什么时候.

1. 桃树(táo)_____开花？ 桃树<u>春天</u>开花。
   peach

2. 学校_____放假？ 学校<u>六月</u>放假。

3. _____？
   小宝宝<u>一岁多</u>会说话。

106

最常用字
Sight Words

zhe
aspect particle 着 着 着

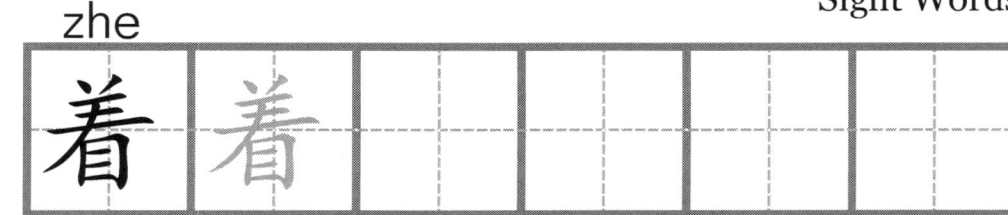

Verb+着 is used to express an ongoing state (-ing). Complete the words with 着.

走___ 等___ 唱___歌 拉___手
walking waiting(děng) singing a song holding hands

谁是谁？Find out who's who and write down the names.

竹青戴(dài)着眼镜。　　文西打着雨伞。
牛牛戴着帽子。　　　　阿乐抱着足球。

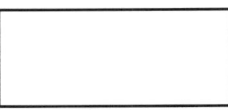

107

Write a sentence about each picture. Use 着.

1. ___开___。

2. ___亮___。

3. 老师站___，
学生坐___。

Read and draw.

1. 天下着雪，yòu又快黑了。一个光着脚(bare feet)的小女孩，在路上慢慢地走着。

2. 家里灯亮着，桌上放着饭和菜。炉(lú)子里生着火，电视也开着。fireplace

108

最常用字
Sight Words

过 — aspect particle

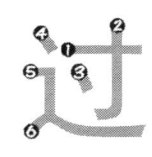

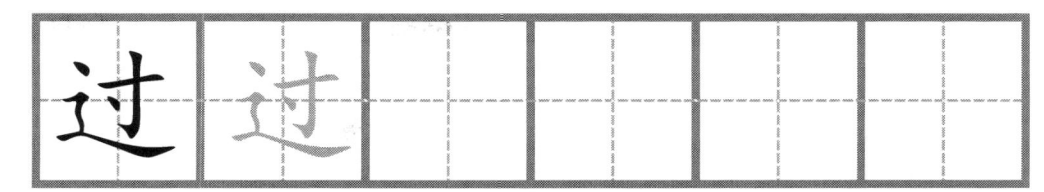

Verb + 过 + Object is used to express an experience (have been/ have done). Fill in the blanks with 过.

我去过中国，坐＿＿火车，看见＿＿熊猫。

If something didn't happen in the past, add 没(有) before the verb. Fill in the blanks with 没(有)...过.

奶奶没有上过大学，也＿＿＿＿＿坐＿＿飞机。

Now draw and write about your experience with 过.

我吃过＿＿＿＿＿＿。   我没有学过＿＿＿＿＿＿。

109

Answer these questions in a complete sentence. Use 过 or 没有...过.

你玩过这个游戏吗?
A: 我玩过这个游戏。
B: 我没有玩过这个游戏。

1. 你坐过飞机吗?

   _____。

2. 你看见过下雪吗?

   _____。

3. 你吃过黄色的西瓜吗?

   _____。

4. 你数过星星吗?

   _____。

最常用字
Sight Words

过…了 indicates that an action is already done. (often for everyday activities like brushing teeth and taking a shower.) Read the story and fill in the blanks with 过…了.

兔妈妈有三只又可爱又听话的小兔子。一天晚上，兔妈妈出门去拔(bá)萝卜，叫小兔子们自己在家吃饭、扫地、洗澡，还要刷牙。

一会儿，兔妈妈回来了。她问小兔子："你们吃过饭了吗？＿＿＿＿＿＿了吗？＿＿＿＿＿＿了吗？＿＿＿＿＿＿了吗？"

小兔子们回答(dá)说："我们吃过饭了，＿＿＿＿＿了，＿＿＿＿＿了，也＿＿＿＿＿了！"

兔妈妈说，"宝贝们，你们太棒(bàng)了！"
awesome

111

不过 is used as a softer "but" or "however".
Complete the sentences with 不过.

1. 我去过中国，_____没去看大熊猫。

2. 加拿大很好玩，_____冬天去太冷了。
   Canada

3. 这个字有点儿难，_____我认识。
   nán
   difficult

4. 河水有点儿凉，_____我们可以划船。
   kě yǐ
   can

5. 学校有点儿远，_____。

6. 这件衣服好漂亮，_____。

最常用字
Sight Words

again, once again, also

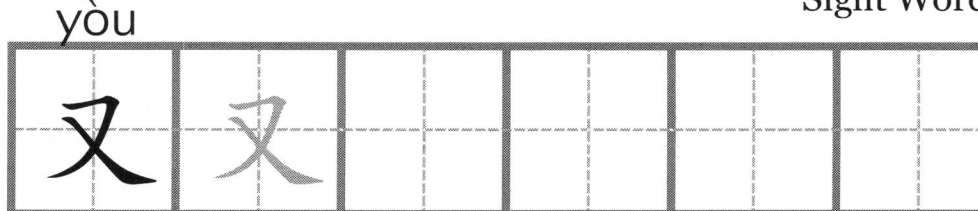

yòu
又 | 又 | 叉 | | | |

Fill in the blanks with 又.

1. 过年了，我___长大了一岁。

2. 家门口的小树___长高了。

3. 昨天下雨，今天___下雨。

又…又… means "both... and...". Complete the sentences with 又…又…. Use the words in the parenthesis.

1. 中秋的月亮_____，真漂亮。
   （大　圆）

2. 小朋友们_____，真开心。
   （唱　跳）

3. 弟弟的眼睛_____，像两个黑葡萄。
   　　　　　　　　　　　xiàng　　　pú táo
   （黑　亮）　　　　　look like

4. 大黄狗_____，是我的好朋友。
   （聪明　　勇敢）

113

Read, answer, and draw. 画一画。

1. 什么动物又高又瘦？
 _____长颈鹿(jǐng lù)_____。

2. 什么动物又抓老鼠、又吃鱼？
 _____。

3. 什么动物又在地上跳、又在水里游？
 _____。

4. 什么水果又大又甜？
 _____。

最常用字
Sight Words

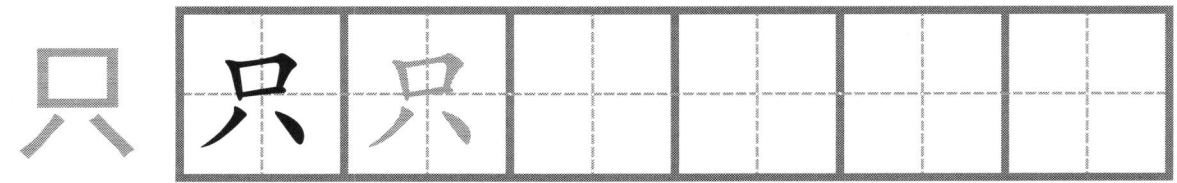

1. measure word
2. only

只

Complete the words and sentences with 只.

I. 只(zhī) as a measure word

一___鞋   ___   ___   ___

II. 只(zhǐ) meaning "only"

1. 今晚___看见星星，看不见月亮。

2. 弟弟___爱吃糖，长(zhǎng)了好多虫牙。
   grow

3. 我___学过一年中文。

4. 妹妹___比我小一岁。

5. 做冰棍(gùn)___放糖，不放盐(yán)。
   popsicle   salt

115

只好 means "have to". Fill in the blanks with 只好.

1. 书店还没有开门，我们____在门口等。

2. 今天又下雨，____下个星期再去动物园了。

3. 爸爸的车坏了，他____坐公交车(jiāo)上班。

Complete the sentences with the following "只" words.

只想   只会   只有   只好   只爱

1. 我____一个哥哥，没有姐妹。

2. 外公____说中文，不会说英文。

3. 爸爸上了一天班，累得(lèi de)____躺(tǎng)下。
   so tired that

4. 妹妹____画画，不爱唱歌。

5. 妈妈忘了带(dài)钥匙(yào shi)，____打电话给警察(jǐng chá)。
   bring

最常用字
Sight Words

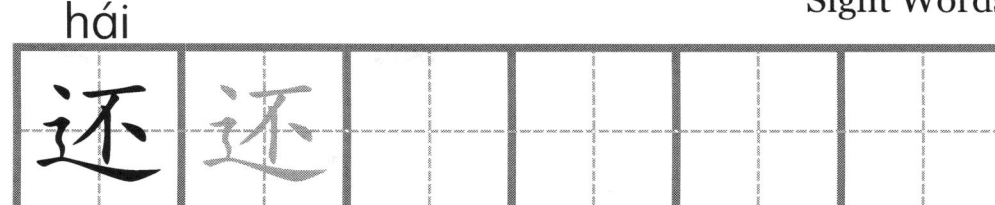

hái
还

1. still
2. also

I. 还 means "still". Fill in the blanks with 还.

1. 今天下雨，明天___下雨。

2. 妹妹学了一年游泳，___没学会。

3. 九点了，你怎么___不睡觉？

还有 means "still have left". Write Math problems with 还有, and answer the questions.

1. 问：一张披萨(pī sà)分成八块，妹妹吃了一块，_____几块？

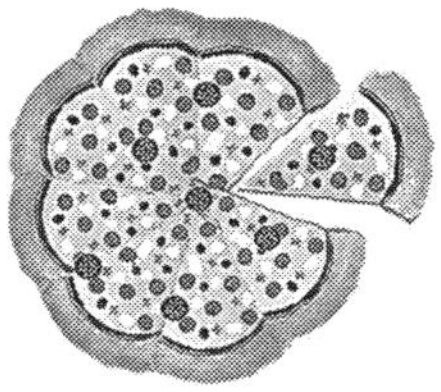

    答：_____。

2. 问：地上有七只鸟，两只飞到了树上，地上_____几只？

    答：_____。

117

II. 还 means "also". Fill in the blanks with 还.

1. 去年夏天我去了中国，学会了很多中国话，___认识了很多新朋友。

2. 我会说中文、写中文，___会唱中文歌。

还是 **in a question** offers a choice, meaning "or". Complete these questions with 还是.

1. 你想喝牛奶_____喝橙汁？

2. 今天放学后，你想踢球_____画画？

3. 你更喜欢吃中国饭_____美国饭？

还是 **in a statement** offers a better choice, meaning "had better". Complete these statements with 还是.

1. 天要黑了，我们_____早点回家吧。

2. 快要下雨了，你_____把伞带上吧。

3. 今天太热了，_____明天再去爬山吧。

最常用字
Sight Words

huò
或

或者
or

zhě
者

Fill in the blanks with 或者.

1. 请用黑色笔_____蓝色笔写。

2. 请在下个星期二_____星期三来。

3. 女生可以穿裤子_____裙子。
   kě yǐ

4. 我想种一棵桃树_____一棵苹果树。
   táo   píng

5. 我想养一个宠物，猫_____狗都行。
   yǎng   chǒng   okay
   raise, grow pet

6. 请让你的爸爸_____妈妈给我打个电话。

119

When offering choices, 还是 is used in questions while 或者 is used in statements. Fill in the blanks. Use 还是 in questions and 或者 in answers.

1. A: 你哪天有时间来我家玩？
   B: 这个星期六_____星期天。

2. A: 做完作业你想玩什么？
   B: 踢足球_____打篮球。

3. A: 你是不小心_____故意的？
   B: 对不起，我不是故意的。

4. A: 你要草莓冰淇淋_____香草冰淇淋？
   B: 巧克力_____香草都可以。

5. A: 你喜欢红色_____蓝色？
   B: 我喜欢红色。

最常用字
Sight Words

néng
can, able to 能

I. 能 tells about ability. Fill in the blanks with 能.

1. 我___吃十个饺子。

2. 我们都___说一些中文。

3. 骆驼不怕渴，___走过沙漠。
   mò
   desert

4. 老鹰的眼睛很好，___看见很远的东西。
   yīng
   eagle

II. 能 can also indicate possibility. Fill in the blanks with 能.

1. 爸爸明天下午___到家吗？

2. 宝宝睡觉了，___小点声说话吗？
   shēng

3. 你___跟我一起玩吗？

4. 大象___活六十年。
   huó
   live

121

不能 means "can't" or "shouldn't". Make your own sentences with 不能.

1. 上课的时候，不能_____。

2. 开车的时候，不能_____。

3. 今天下雨了，不能_____。

4. 弟弟牙疼，不能_____。

可能 means "probably" or "possibly", and 不可能 means "impossible". Fill in the blanks with 可能 or 不可能.

1. 今天好冷，_____要下雪了。

2. 太阳_____从西边出来。

3. 雨过天晴的时候_____会看见彩虹。
   cǎi hóng

4. 我听到停车的声音，_____是爸爸回来了。

5. 鱼_____生活在树上。

122

最常用字
Sight Words

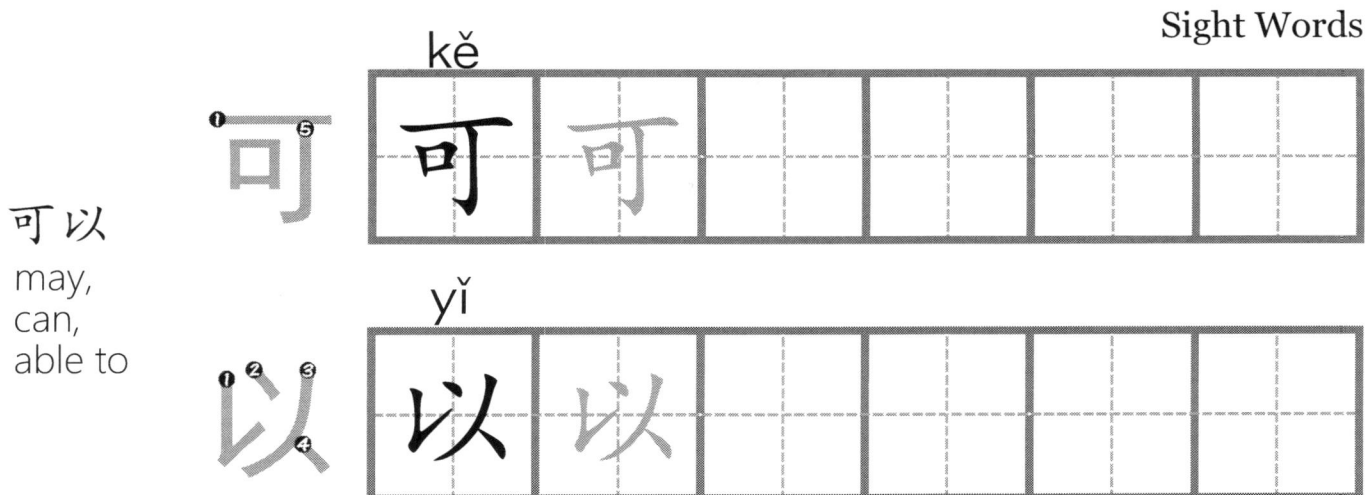

kě
可

可以
may, can, able to

yǐ
以

I. Express ability. Fill in the blanks with 可以.

1. 骆驼_____十多天不吃不喝。

2. 蛇_____吞下比自己大很多的动物。
   tūn
   swallow

3. 姐姐十二岁，_____自己一个人在家了。
   jǐ
   self

4. 哥哥十六岁，_____学开车了。

II. Express permission or possibility.

1. 我_____进来吗？

2. 我_____坐在这里吗？

3. 我_____喝一杯果汁吗？

4. 你_____去院子里玩一会儿。

123

不可以 means "can't" or "not allowed". Make sentences with 不可以.

1. 这个游泳池很浅，<u>不可以跳水</u>。

2. 地上很滑，_____。
   (huá / slippery)

3. 在图书馆里，_____。
   (guǎn / library)

4. 吃饭的时候，_____。

能 and 可以 are interchangeable in many cases. Fill in the blanks with 能 or 可以. Either one will work just fine.

1. 我的腿疼，今天不____游泳了。

2. 面粉____做成面包、面条和饼干。

3. 妈妈，我____吃一个甜甜圈吗？

4. 不____随便坐陌生人的车。
   (suí biàn)

5. 每个人都要说真话，不____说假话。

最常用字
Sight Words

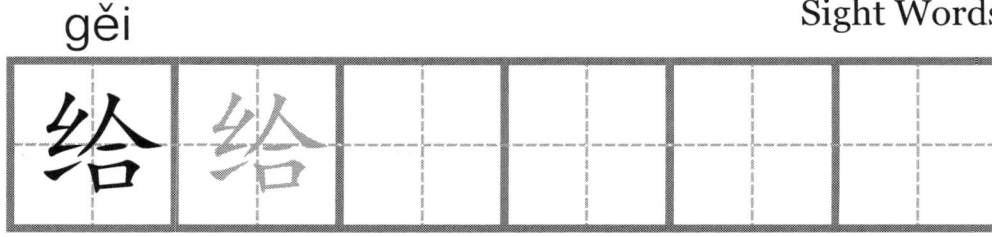

gěi
给 给 给

give

I. 给 means to give or to provide. Complete the sentences with 给.

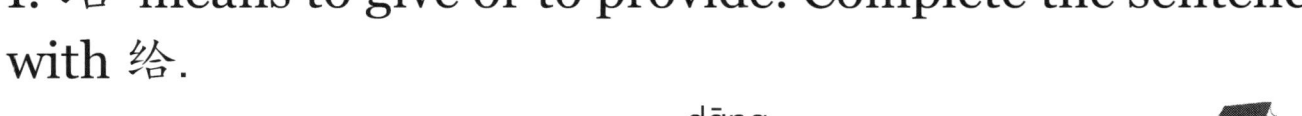

1. 爸爸___我一本书当(dāng)生日礼物。

2. 好朋友___了我一个大大的拥(yōng)抱。

3. 外婆___我一个大红包。
red envelope (with gift money in it)

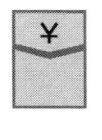

II. 给 also means to do something for someone. Complete these sentences.

1. 医生___病人看病，护士(hù shi)___病人打针。
nurse

2. 妈妈___我做饭，我给妈妈_____。

3. 爸爸___我讲故事，我给爸爸_____。

4. 家里来客(kè)人了，我给客人_____。

5. 吃饭的时候，我给大家_____。

125

Quiz Time!

Fill in the blanks with characters from the box.

| 先 再 着 过 只 又 还 给 |

1. 弟弟天不怕地不怕，___是怕蛇。
   fear nothing in heaven or on earth

2. 半夜十二点了，爸爸还在忙___工作。
   work

3. 谁也没有看见___风。
   Nobody has ever seen

4. 北极熊会游泳，___会抓鱼。

5. 回家后，我想___吃饭，___做作业。

6. 我___小花狗起个名字叫斑比。

7. 黑夜里的星星___大___亮。

Look at the pictures and make sentences with 很，更，最.

地球　　　　　　　土星　　　　　　　木星

_____，_____，_____。

Complete the sentences with 还是，或者，可以，or 可能.

1. 写完作业后，我想打球_____弹琴。

2. 你_____先吃些点心再写作业。

3. 不知道明天会下雨_____会天晴？

4. 明天_____会有小雨。

句型结构
Sentence Structure

Subject + Verb

句型结构
Sentence Structure

你　看。

Pick a word from each category to make sentences.

Subject

春天　百花

太阳　鸟儿

鱼儿　公鸡

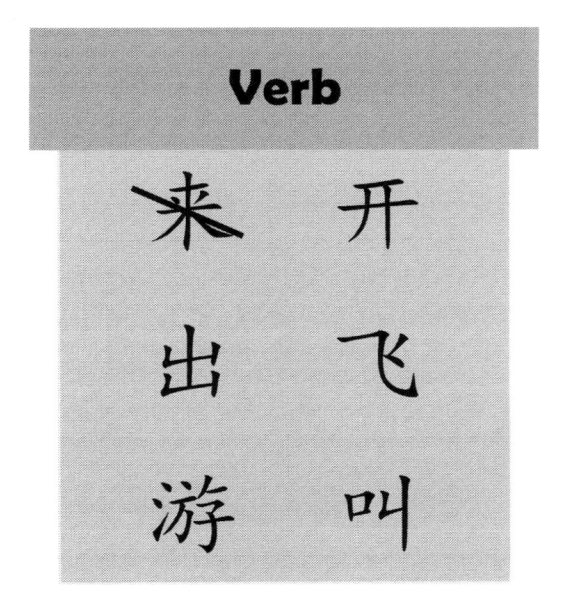

Verb

来　开

出　飞

游　叫

1. 春天 __来__ ，_____ 开。

2. _____ 飞，_____ 游。

3. 公鸡 ____，_____ 出。

Read these sentences. Draw a △ around the subject and a ▢ around the verb.

1. 爸爸 看。

2. 妈妈 听。

3. 微风 吹。

4. 小树 摇。
    yáo
    sway

129

Look at the pictures and write **Subject + Verb** sentences.

吃　落　爬　闪　哭　沉　浮

1. 大风吹。

2. _____。

3. _____。

4. _____。

5. _____。

6. _____。

7. _____。

8. _____。

Subject + Adjective

月亮　　弯。

Pick a word from each category to make sentences.

句型结构
Sentence Structure

Subject

冬天	小道
走路	石头
夏天	羽毛
马路	开车

Adjective

宽	热
慢	窄
冷	重
快	轻

1. _____, _____。

2. _____, _____。

3. _____, _____。

4. _____, _____。

131

Read these sentences. Draw a △ around the subject and a ⏢ around the adjective.

1. 花儿 火红。
2. 云儿 雪白。
3. 弟弟 认真。
3. 哥哥 勇敢。

Look at the pictures and write **Subject+Adjective** sentences.

长　空　满　疼　脏

1. 尾巴_____。

2. 电池_____。

3. _____。

4. 衣服_____。

5. _____。

Subject + Verb + Object

句型结构
Sentence Structure

我 吃 饭。

Pick a word from each category to make sentences.

谁	做	什么
小猫 她	坐 玩	球 火车
男孩 羊	说 吃	中文 书
他们 鸡	看 骑	马 虫子

1.  小猫看书。

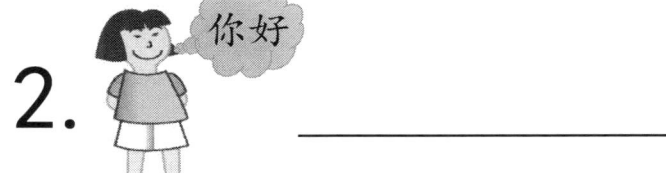

2. _____。

3.  _____。

4. _____。

5.  _____。

6. _____。

133

谁做什么? Ask a question about the underlined words with 谁/什么.

谁打篮球?   冰冰打篮球。
冰冰打什么?   冰冰打篮球。

1. _____?   小猫钓鱼。
   _____?   小猫钓鱼。

2. _____?   妹妹吹气球。
   _____?   妹妹吹气球。

3. _____?   奶奶种花。
   _____?   奶奶种花。

4. _____?   妈妈做蛋糕。
   _____?   妈妈做蛋糕。

Subject + Time + Verb Phrase

句型结构
Sentence Structure

我　早上七点　起床。

Read these time words.

哪一年	什么季节	哪个月 几月	哪个星期	哪一天 星期几	几点	
去年 今年 明年 后年 2018 年 每年	春天 夏天 秋天 冬天	上个月 这个月 下个月 一月 每个月	上个星期 这个星期 下个星期 每个星期	前天 昨天 今天 明天 后天 星期三	早上 上午 中午 下午 晚上 半夜	六点 九点零五 十二点半 三点四十 七点一刻

Fill in the blanks with a time word to complete the sentences.

谁   **什么时候**   **做什么**

1. 妈妈 　_____　 不上班 。
2. 我们家 　_____　 吃晚饭 。
3. 我 　_____　 过生日 。
4. 树叶 　_____　 落下 。
5. 猫头鹰 (yīng) (owl) 　_____　 不睡觉 。

135

Answer the questions with a time word.

1. 问：花儿什么季jì节开？

   答：花儿<u>春天</u>开。

2. 问：美国人每年几月过感恩节？

   答：美国人_____过感恩节。

3. 问：你们班星期几有tǐ yù kè体育课？

   答：我们班_____有体育课。

4. 问：你的生日是几月几号？

   答：我的生日是_____。

5. 问：你晚上几点睡觉？

   答：我_____睡觉。

136

Subject + Place + Verb Phrase

句型结构
SENTENCE STRUCTURE

我　　在家　　睡觉。

Fill in the blanks with a location word to complete the sentences.

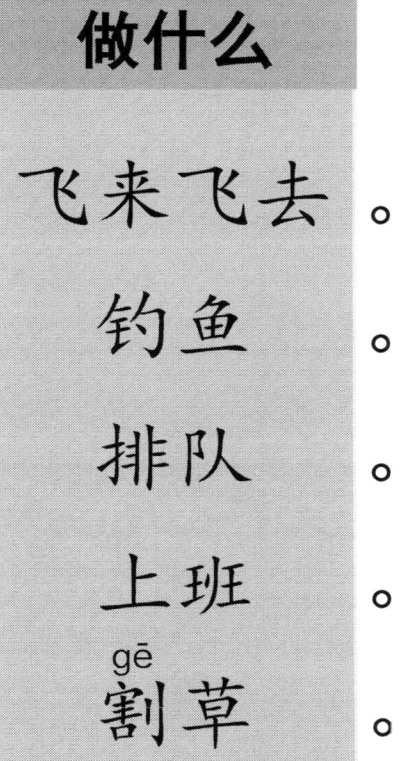

谁	在哪儿	做什么
1. 蜻蜓	_____	飞来飞去。
2. 爷爷	_____	钓鱼。
3. 人们	_____	排队。
4. 医生	_____	上班。
5. 工人	_____	ᵍᵉ割草。

在花园里

在饭店门口

在河边

在医院

在路边

137

Subject + Verb★ + 在 + Place A small group of special verbs that imply movement or location can be used before 在. Remember that not all verbs can be used this way.

一只蝴蝶<u>停在</u>大象的鼻子上。

Fill in the blanks with a special **verb★** +在.

走　　生活　　骑　　长　　照

1. 老鼠＿＿＿马背上。

2. 狐狸和黑熊都＿＿＿森林里。

3. 老虎＿＿＿山间的小路上。

4. 阳光＿＿＿海面上。

5. 香蕉(jiāo)＿＿＿香蕉树上。

句型结构
Sentence Structure

Subject + Time + Place + Verb Phrase

我　星期六　去学校　打篮球。

Use the picture clue to complete these sentences.

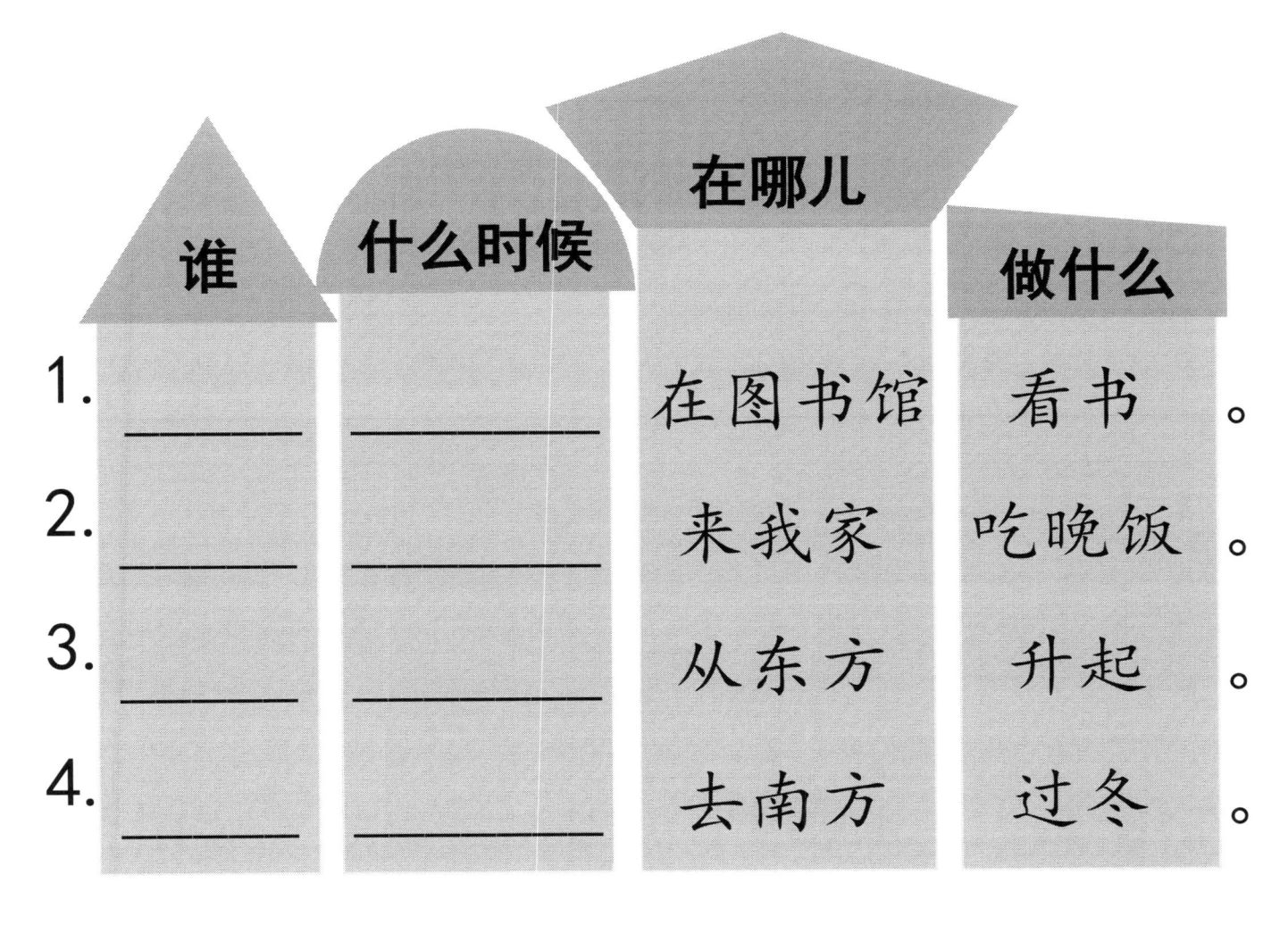

谁	什么时候	在哪儿	做什么
1. _____	_____	在图书馆	看书 。
2. _____	_____	来我家	吃晚饭 。
3. _____	_____	从东方	升起 。
4. _____	_____	去南方	过冬 。

太阳
每天早上

yàn
燕子
每年冬天

邻居一家
星期六

王老师
现在

139

Rearrange the words in this order to make sentences.

Subject + Time + Place + Verb Phrase

1. 早上七点 在家 我 吃早饭

   _____。

2. 星期六 去公园 外公 放风筝

   _____。

3. 哥哥 拿信 每天下午 去邮箱

   _____。

4. 放学后 在车库门口 打球 我的邻居

   _____。

5. 在中国 去年 我 学会了用筷子

   _____。

Subject + Adverb + Verb Phrase

句型结构
Sentence Structure

小鸟　开心地　吃玉米。

Pick a word from each category to make sentences.

谁	怎样地	做什么
青蛙	轻轻地	游
小雨	呱呱地	下
微风	沙沙地 (sound of rain)	吹
鱼儿	快乐地	叫

1. _____。

2. _____。

3. _____。

4. _____。

Choose an adverb from the box to describe the verb in each sentence. A hint is given in English.

| 飞快地 | 慢吞吞地 | 远远地 | 细心地 |
| 着急地 | 勇敢地 | 吃惊地 | 快乐地 |

1. 金鱼在水里_____吐着泡泡。(happily)

2. 蜗牛_____往树上爬。(slowly)
   (wō) snail

3. 火车_____开过。(fast, quickly)

4. 从这里可以_____看到山下。(far)

5. 消防员_____把大火扑灭了。(bravely)
   (xiāo fáng yuán) / (pū miè) extinguish

6. 姐姐_____把礼物包好。(carefully)

7. 钥匙丢了,弟弟_____到处找。
   (diū) lost / (anxiously) / (chù) everywhere

8. 听到这,大家都_____看着他。
   (surprisedly)

句型结构
Sentence Structure

Topic-comment sentences.

The topic of a sentence is sometimes placed in the beginning for emphasizing. Rewrite the sentences. Put the underlined words at the beginning of each sentence.

Topic	Comment
这裙子	你穿真漂亮。
	大家都爱吃。
	有吗？

你穿<u>这裙子</u>真漂亮。 ➡

大家都爱吃<u>饺子</u>。 ➡

有<u>一块钱</u>吗？ ➡

Rearrange the word order to make topic-comment sentences.

1. 我认识<u>这个字</u>。 ➡ _____。

2. 老虎不吃<u>青菜</u>。 ➡ _____。

3. 你会<u>做饭</u>吗？ ➡ _____？

4. 大家不怕<u>下雨</u>。 ➡ _____。

5. 做完<u>作业</u>了吗？ ➡ _____？

Draw and write your comment on each topic.

这双鞋<u>太贵(guì)了</u>。
too expensive

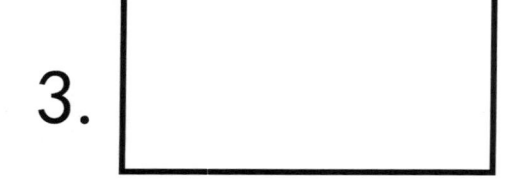

1. 这里的夏天_____。

2. 我家的后院_____。

3. 妈妈做的饭_____。

4. 地里的胡萝卜_____。

5. 新买的自行车_____。

Fun Time!

1. Shade the word cards by this code:

   | 谁=红色 | 什么时候=黄色 | 在哪儿=蓝色 | 做什么=绿色 |

2. Cut out the cards, and sort them into 4 piles by the color.

3. Each player draws a card from each pile, and arrange the words to make a sentence. Then read it aloud.

在花盆里	兔子和乌龟	在座位底下	圣诞老人
我的邻居	在蹦蹦床上	昨天早上	讲故事
骑毛驴	半夜十二点	小的时候	在月亮上
在烟囱里	弹吉他	警察叔叔	切面包
排队买饭	去年冬天	在车库里	我的朋友
我的爸爸	白雪公主	上个星期	每天中午
今年一月	在铅笔盒里	抓痒	煮鸡蛋

人文
People and Culture

Continents and Oceans

人文
People and Culture

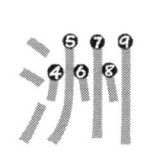

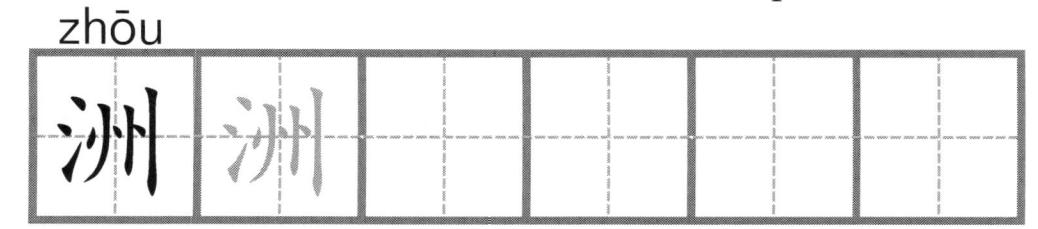

continent zhōu 洲 洲 洲

ocean yáng 洋 洋 洋

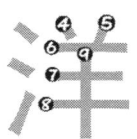

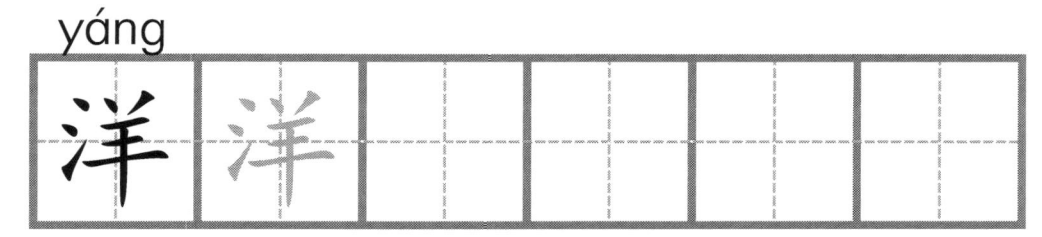

Fill in the blanks with 洲 and say the 7 continents in the world.

ōu
欧___
Europe

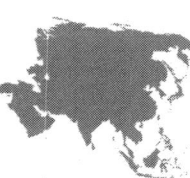

yà
亚___
Asia

fēi
非___
Africa

北美___
North America

南美___
South America

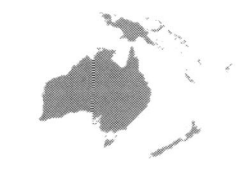

大洋___
Oceania

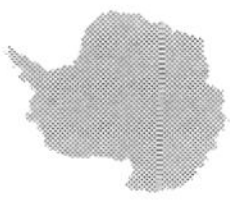

jí
南极___
Antarctica

147

Fill in the blanks with 洋 and say the 5 oceans in the world.

北冰___ Arctic Ocean

大西___ Atlantic Ocean

太平___ Pacific Ocean

yìn dù
印度___ Indian Ocean

南冰___ Southern (Antarctic) Ocean

Fill in the blanks with words in the box.

中国　北美洲　北冰洋　地球

_____上有五大洋、七大洲。五大洋是太平洋、大西洋、印度洋、南冰洋和_____。七大洲是欧洲、亚洲、非洲、_____、南美洲、大洋洲和南极洲。_____是亚洲最大的国家。

Population

People and Culture
人文

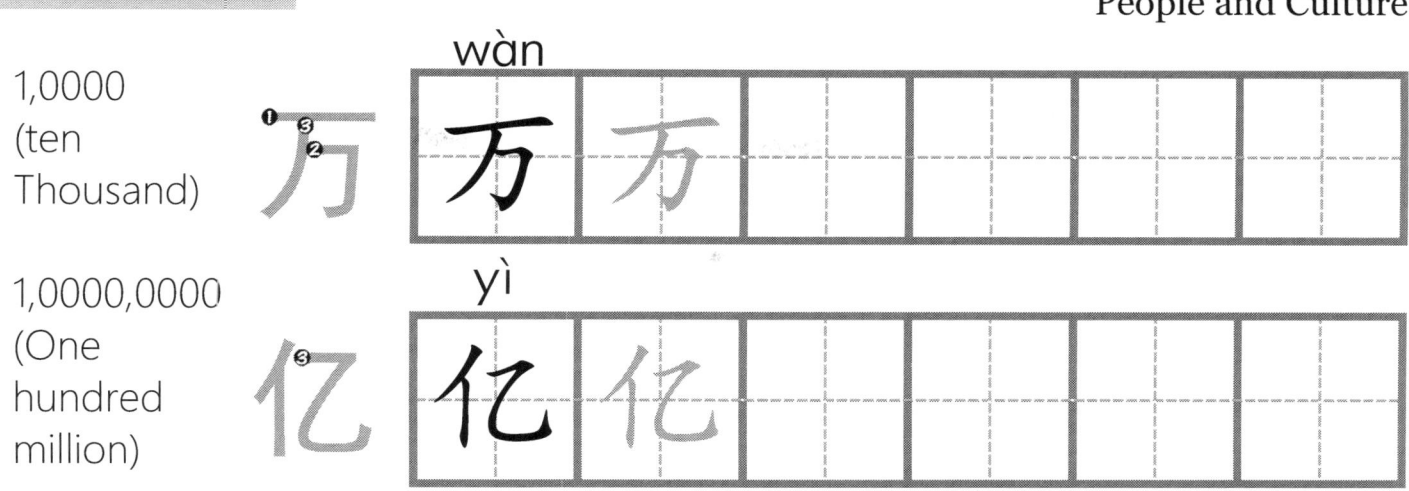

1,0000
(ten Thousand)

wàn
万 万

1,0000,0000
(One hundred million)

yì
亿 亿

Place value in Chinese. A comma is written for every four digits starting from the ones' place.

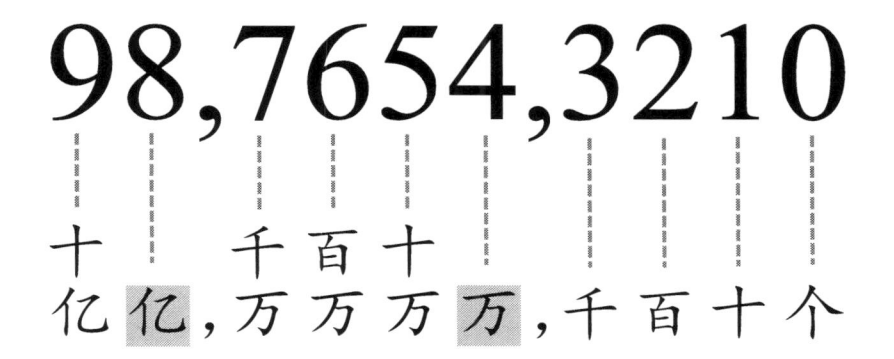

98,7654,3210

十 千百十
亿 亿 , 万 万 万 万 , 千 百 十 个

This number is read as:

九十八亿, 七千六百五十四万, 三千二百一十

Try it. Write how you would read this number in Chinese.

75,8124,6390

149

Underline the numbers in the words and then write them down under their place values in the chart.

1. <u>十三</u>亿<u>八</u>千<u>四</u>百<u>四十一</u>万<u>三</u>千<u>七</u>百<u>七十一</u>
2. 十三亿四千零(líng)四十九万两千七百零七
3. 三亿两千六百零九万

十亿	亿	千万	百万	十万	万	千	百	十	个
1	3	8	4	4	1	3	7	7	1

1.
2.
3.

Fill in the blanks with words in the word box.

亿　千万　百万　国家

中国的人口有十三亿八＿＿＿，是世界(shì jiè)上人口最多的＿＿＿。印度(yìn dù)的人口有十三＿＿＿四千万，是世界上人口第二(dì)多的＿＿＿。美国的人口有三亿两千六＿＿＿，是世界上人口第三多的＿＿＿。

150

Languages

人文
People and Culture

language — yǔ 语

words, speech — yán 言

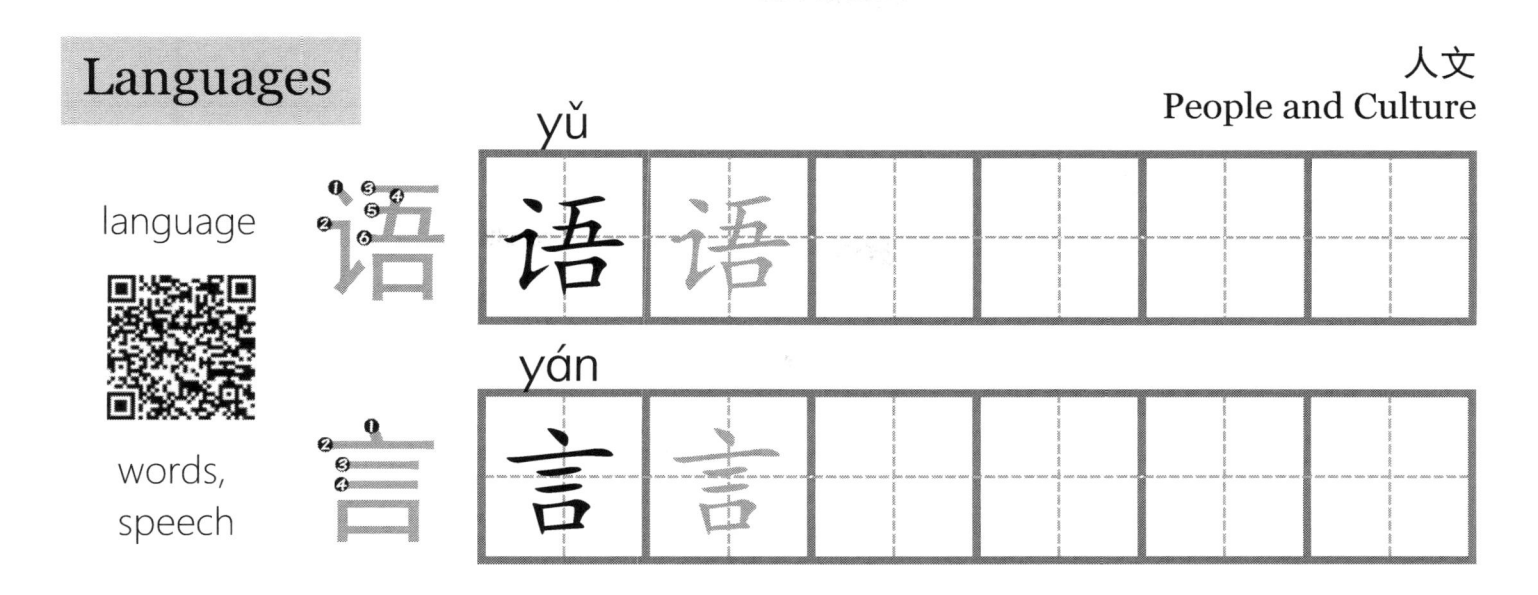

Fill in the blanks with 语 and match the languages with the countries where they are spoken. Some languages are spoken in many countries.

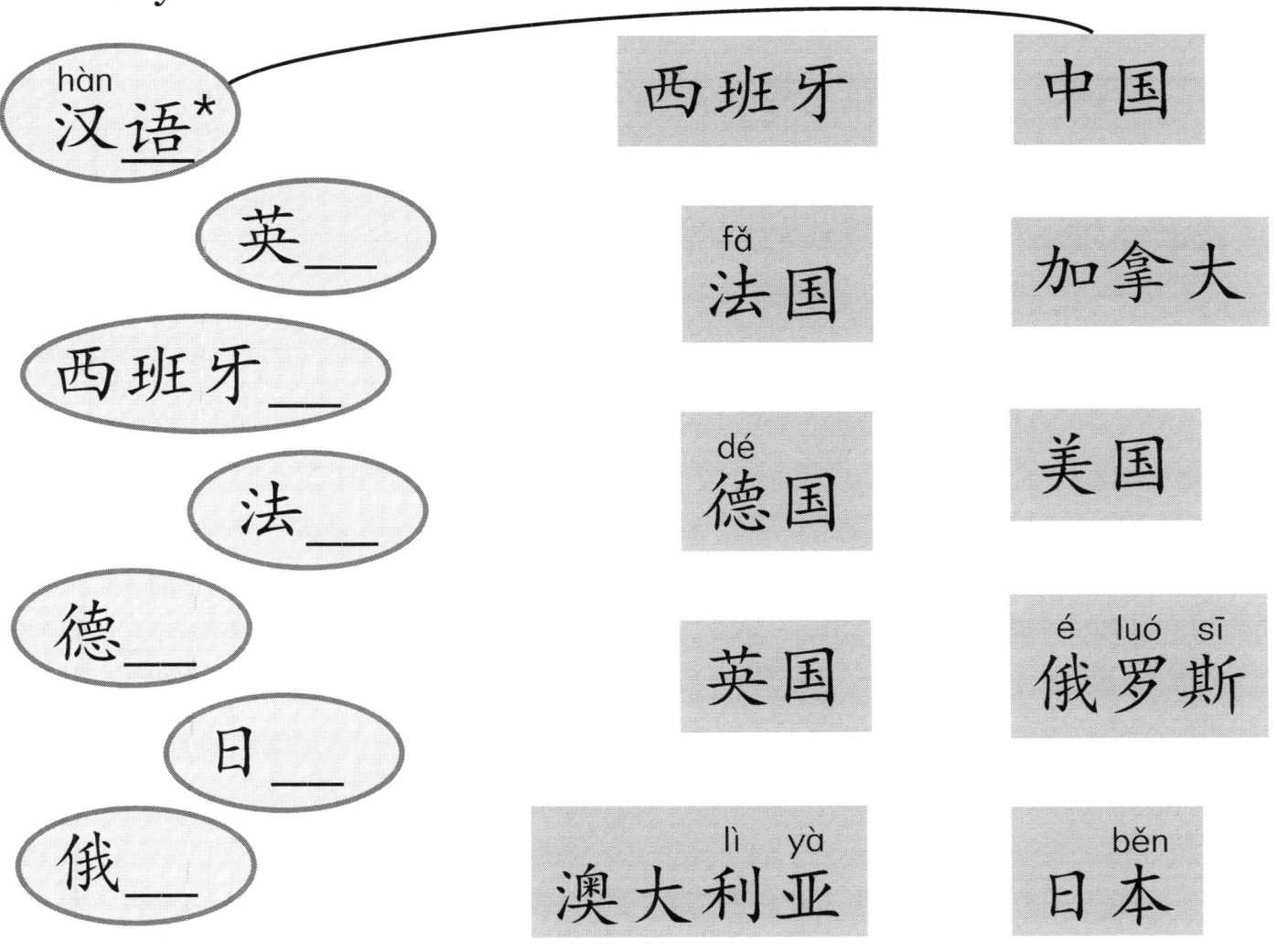

- hàn 汉语*
- 英__
- 西班牙__
- 法__
- 德__
- 日__
- 俄__

西班牙

中国

fǎ 法国

加拿大

dé 德国

美国

英国

é luó sī 俄罗斯

lì yà 澳大利亚

běn 日本

*汉语, "Chinese language", is interchangeable with 中文, "Chinese", in many cases.

Read and answer.

熊文远住在加拿大。他的爸爸是加拿大人，妈妈是中国人。从星期一到星期五，他在学校说英语和法语。星期六和星期天他去中文学校学汉语。

（zhù live）

1. 熊文远会说什么语言？

_____。

2. 你觉得他的妈妈会说什么语言？

（jué de feel, think）

_____。

Write about yourself and the language(s) that you speak.

我叫_____，我住在_____。

我的爸爸是_____人，妈妈是_____人。_____。

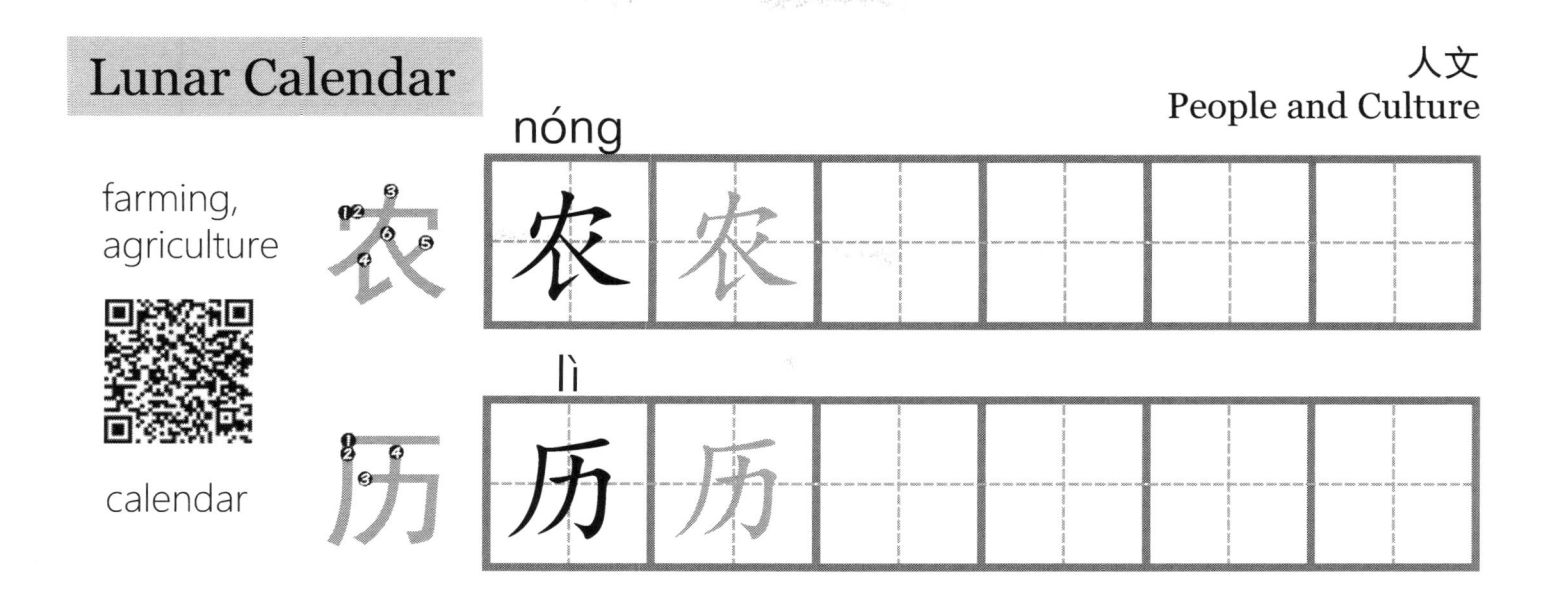

Lunar Calendar

人文
People and Culture

farming, agriculture

nóng
农 农

lì
历 历

calendar

A Chinese Calendar has both the Solar Calendar and the Lunar Calendar on it. A Lunar Calendar month usually has 29 or 30 days.

日	一	二	三	四	五	六
				1 十六	**2** 十七	**3** 十八
4 立春	**5** 二十	**6** 廿一	**7** 廿二	**8** 小年	**9** 廿四	**10** 廿五
11 廿六	**12** 廿七	**13** 廿八	**14** 廿九	**15** 除夕	**16** 春节	**17** 初二
18 初三	**19** 雨水	**20** 初五	**21** 初六	**22** 初七	**23** 初八	**24** 初九
25 初十	**26** 十一	**27** 十二	**28** 十三			

The bold numbers are showing the Solar Calendar and the characters under them are showing the Lunar Calendar. (廿 niàn means 20, 廿一 means 21, etc.)

153

A Lunar Calendar is a calendar that is based on the cycle of the moon's phases. Fill in the missing dates on this calendar.

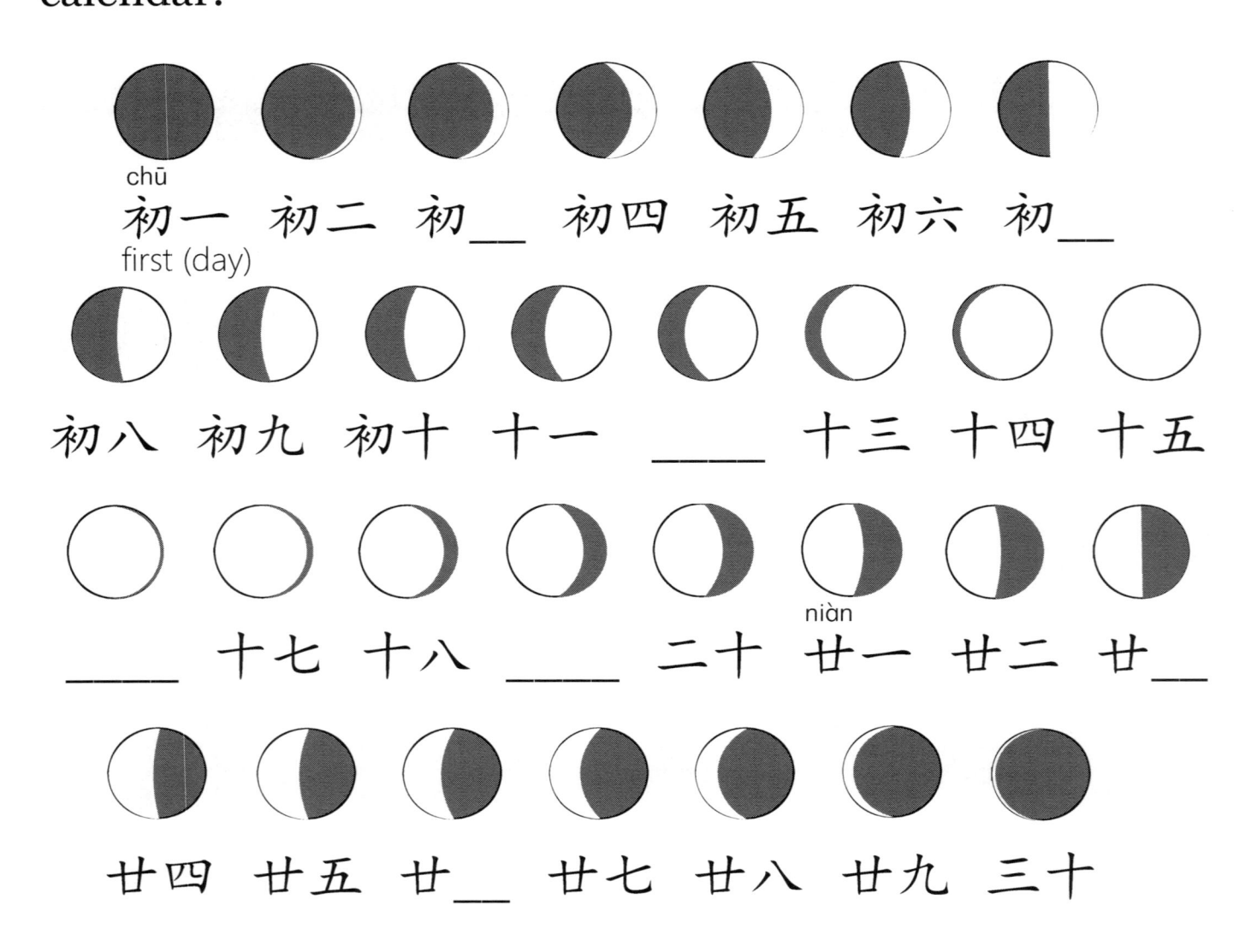

chū
初一 初二 初__ 初四 初五 初六 初__
first (day)

初八 初九 初十 十一 ___ 十三 十四 十五

niàn
___ 十七 十八 ___ 二十 廿一 廿二 廿__

廿四 廿五 廿__ 廿七 廿八 廿九 三十

Look at the moon phases above and answer the questions.

1. 农历的哪一天看不见月亮？

   _____。

2. 哪一天的月亮又大又圆？

   _____。

Festivals   Chinese New Year's Eve   除夕   人文 People and Culture

1. division
2. get rid of

除 — chú

1. evening,
2. eve

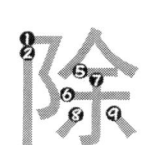

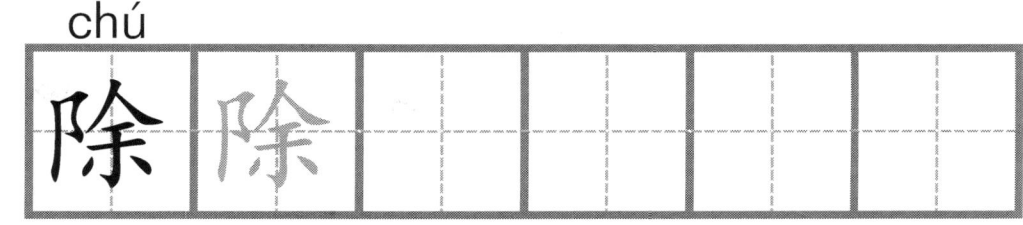

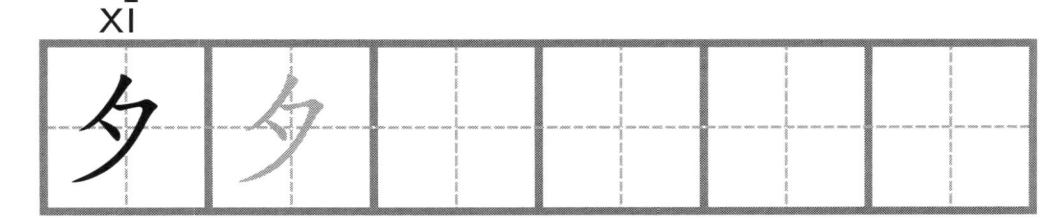

夕 — xī

Read about 除夕 and learn the vocabulary.

除夕是农历十二月三十号，是一年的最后一天，也叫"年三十"。这一天，全家人要坐在一起吃"年夜饭"。人们贴春联(tiē lián)、剪窗花(chuāng)，挂(guà)灯笼(long)，每个人脸上都喜气洋洋(xǐ)。

Vocabulary:

1. 贴春联 — paste the New Year scrolls onto doors

2. 剪窗花 — cut out paper decorations for windows

3. 挂灯笼 — hang up the lanterns

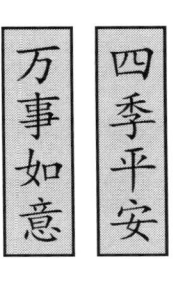

万事如意   四季平安

155

Answer these questions about 除夕.

1. 除夕是农历的几月几号?

   _____。

2. 除夕全家人一起吃的饭叫什么?

   _____。

3. "喜气洋洋" 是什么意思?

   A. 开开心心　　　B. 急急忙忙　　　C. 漂漂亮亮

做纸灯笼 Make a paper lantern. (Adult supervision required.)

You'll need: 牛奶盒、白纸、筷子、绳子、小杯蜡烛(là zhú)、胶水(jiāo)、画笔、剪刀
tealight candle　glue

1. 把牛奶盒的上面剪掉。

2. 画上星星和月亮。

3. 剪下星星和月亮，再在盒子里面贴上纸，把星星和月亮盖住。

4. 把盒子用绳子穿上，再绑(bǎng)上筷子。
tie

5. 里面放上蜡烛，灯笼就做好了！

人文
People and Culture

New Year's Day　　新年

Read about 新年 and learn the vocabulary.

过了年三十的半夜十二点，就是新的一年了。大年初一(chū)是新年的第一(dì)天，小朋友们穿新衣、戴(dài)新帽(mào)，给爷爷奶奶、外公外婆、叔叔(shū)阿姨(ā yí)们拜年(bài)。大人们给小朋友红包，红包里放着"压(yā)岁钱"。过了年，每个人都长大一岁。

Vocabulary:

1. 叔叔 uncle, father's younger brother, men at father's age

2. 拜年 wish happy new year

3. 红包 red envelope

4. 压岁钱 money given to children as a new year's gift

157

Answer these questions about 新年.

1. 新年的第一天是农历的几月几号？

   _____。

2. 新年第一天，小朋友们穿什么？戴什么？

   _____。

3. 小朋友们给谁拜年？
   （bài）

   _____。

4. 大人给小朋友什么？

   _____。

5. "压岁钱"是什么？

   A. 过年的时候，大人给孩子写的信。
   （xìn / letter）

   B. 过年的时候，大人给孩子的钱。

   C. 过生日的时候，大人给孩子的礼物。

人文
People and Culture

The Chinese zodiac 十二生肖(xiāo)

shǔ
鼠 | 鼠 | 鼠 | | | | |

hǔ
虎 | 虎 | 虎 | | | | |

tù
兔 | 兔 | 兔 | | | | |

lóng
龙 | 龙 | 龙 | | | | |

hóu
猴 | 猴 | 猴 | | | | |

zhū
猪 | 猪 | 猪 | | | | |

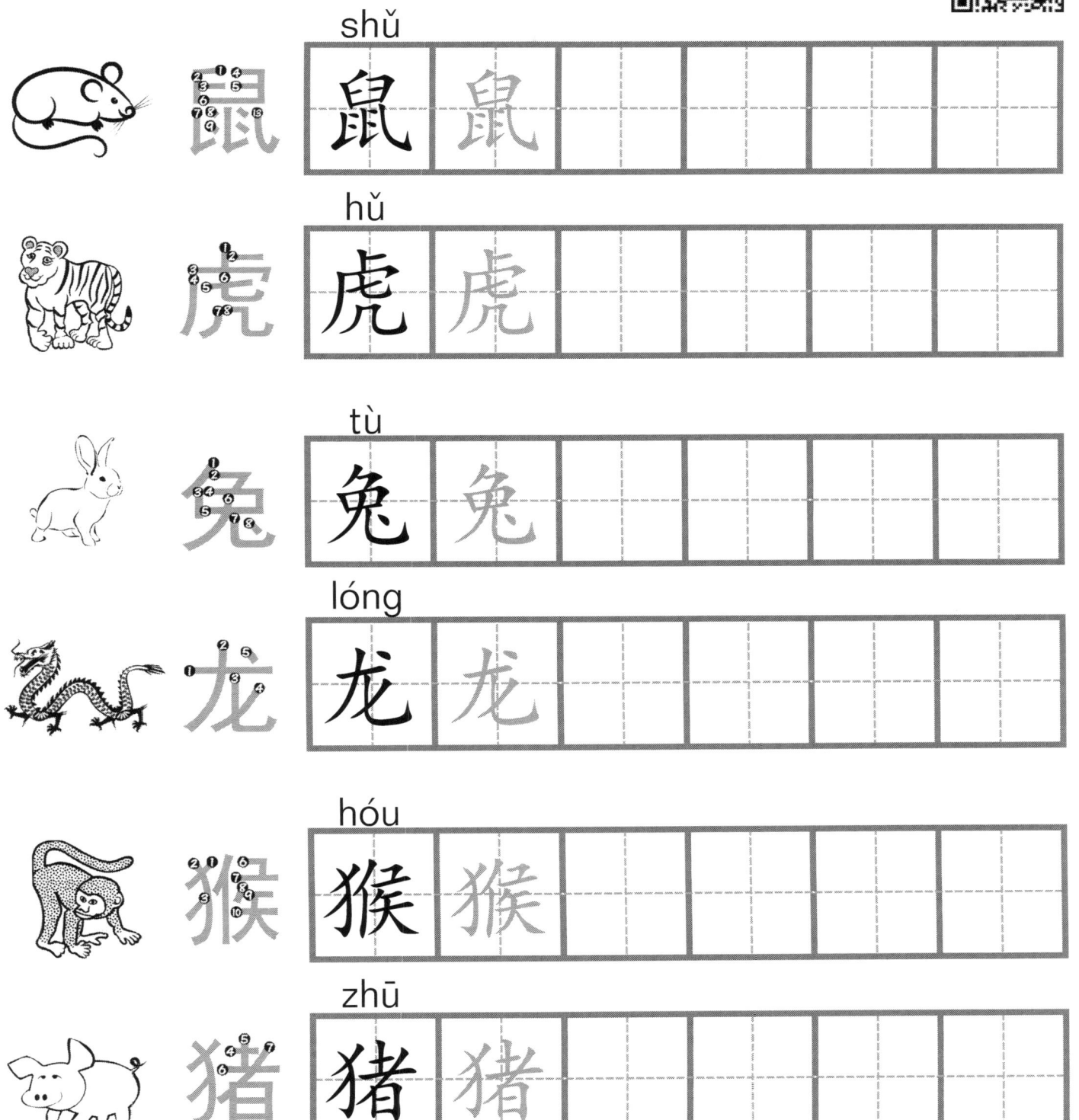

159

Say the names of 十二生肖 and remember them in this order.

鼠 牛 虎 兔 龙 蛇
马 羊 猴 鸡 狗 猪

1948	1949	1950	1951	1952	1953
1960	1961	1962	1963	1964	1965
1972	1973	1974	1975	1976	1977
1984	1985	1986	1987	1988	1989
1996	1997	1998	1999	2000	2001
2008	2009	2010	2011	2012	2013
2020	2021	2022	2023	2024	2025
1954	1955	1956	1957	1958	1959
1966	1967	1968	1969	1970	1971
1978	1979	1980	1981	1982	1983
1990	1991	1992	1993	1994	1994
2002	2003	2004	2005	2006	2007
2014	2015	2016	2017	2018	2019
2026	2027	2028	2029	2030	2031

人文
People and Culture

Check the animal sign for 禾禾, 苗苗, **and their family. Use the chart on the previous page.**

hé　　miáo
禾禾和苗苗的一家

爸爸 1980 年出生，属 <u>猴</u>（born under (animal sign)），今年____岁。妈妈 1983 年出生，属____，今年____岁。禾禾 2010 年出生，属____，今年____岁。苗苗 2013 年出生，属____，今年____岁。

Now draw and write about your family.

Words you may need:

| 爸 妈 哥 姐 弟 妹 爷 奶 外 公 婆 |

我的_____ _____年出生,属____,今年____岁。我的_____ _____年出生,属___,今年_____。我的_____ ____年出生, 属___,今年_____。我_____ _____,属____, _____。

162

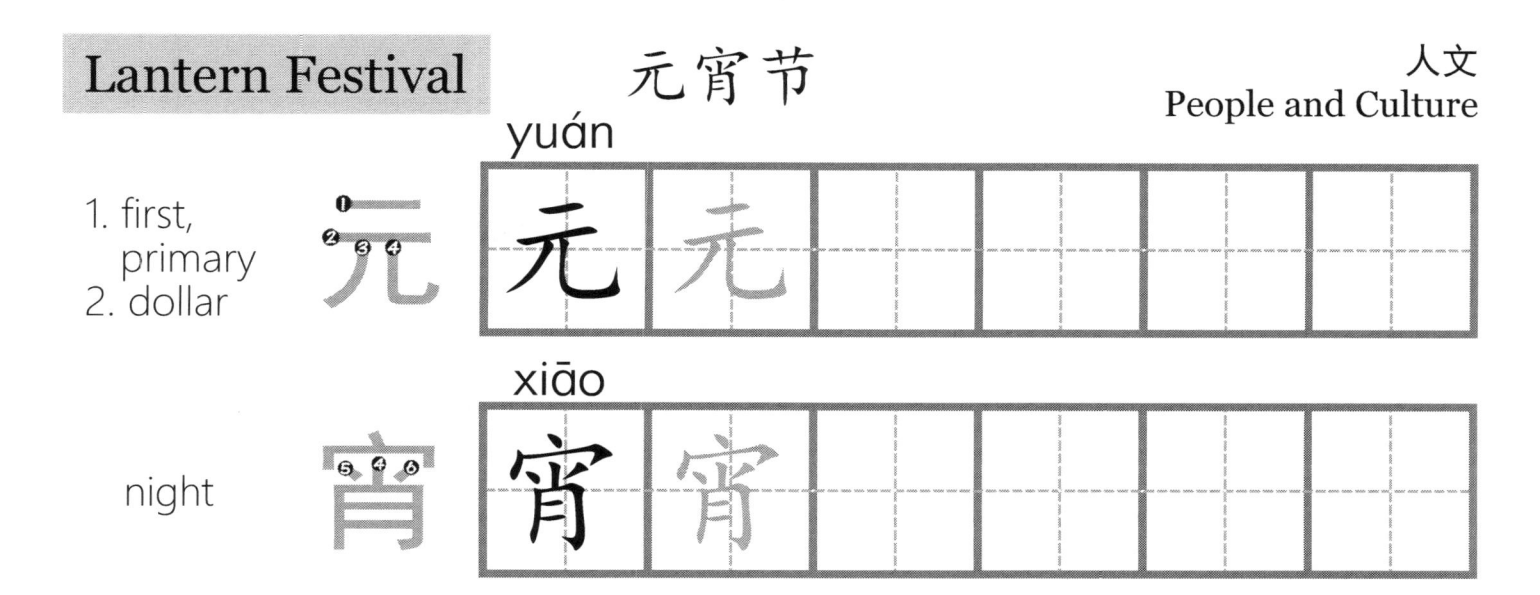

Lantern Festival 元宵节

People and Culture 人文

1. first, primary
2. dollar

yuán
元

night

xiāo
宵

Read about 元宵节 and learn the vocabulary.

<u>zhēng</u>
<u>正月</u>十五是元宵节，也是春节的最后一天。这天，大家吃<u>元宵</u>，看<u>花灯</u>，猜(cāi)<u>灯谜</u>(mí)。过了元宵节，大人上班，小孩上学，又要开始(shǐ)新一年的忙碌(lù)生活。

busy — life
guess
begin

Vocabulary:

1. 正月 — first month of the Lunar year

2. 元宵 — a sticky rice ball with sweet fillings, also called "汤(tāng)圆".

3. 花灯 — lanterns of different shapes

4. 灯谜 — lantern riddles (see next page)

163

猜灯谜，打一字。Can you guess the character for each lantern riddle? Write it on the line.

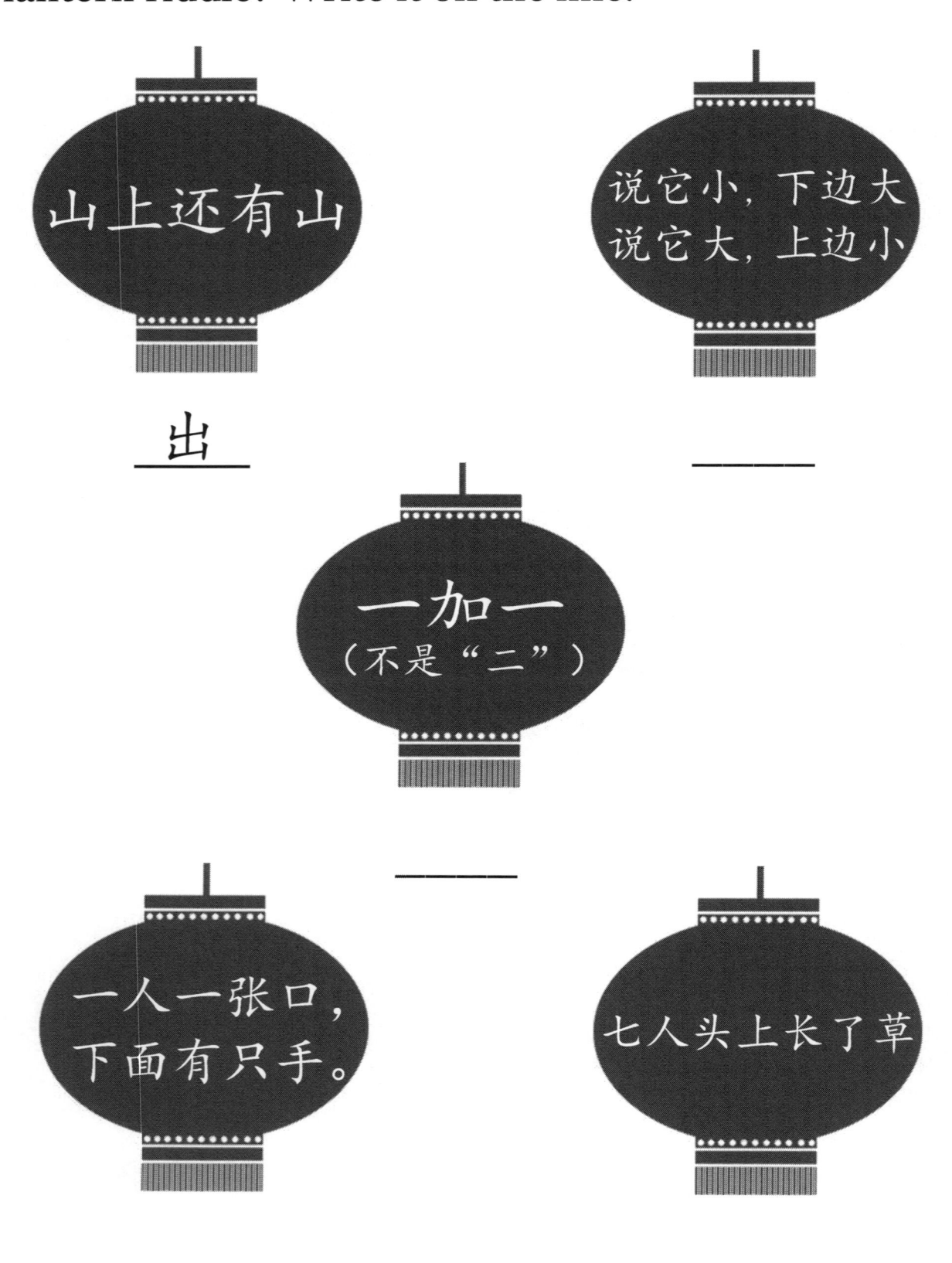

山上还有山

出

说它小，下边大
说它大，上边小

_____

一加一
（不是"二"）

_____

一人一张口，
下面有只手。

_____

七人头上长了草

_____

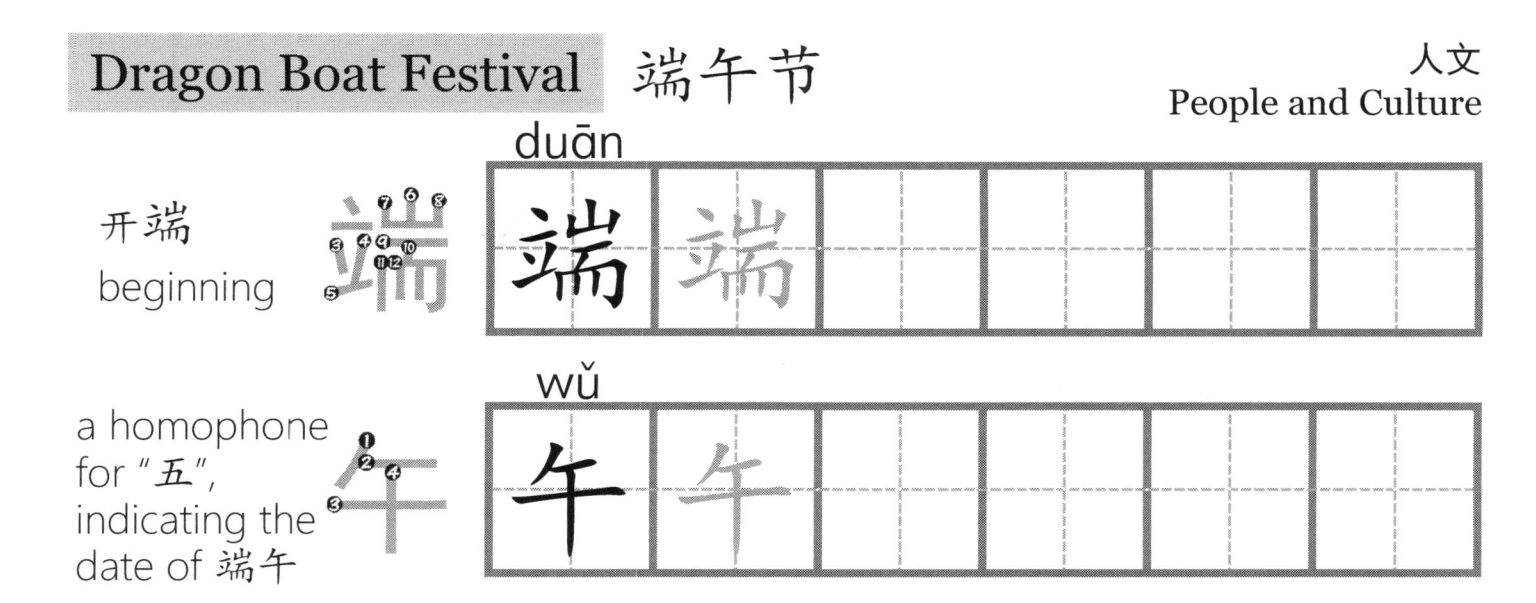

Dragon Boat Festival 端午节

People and Culture 人文

开端
beginning

duān
端 端

wǔ
午 午

a homophone for "五", indicating the date of 端午

Read about 端午节 and learn the vocabulary.

端午是每年农历的五月初五，也叫"五月节"。这一天，人们吃<u>粽子</u>(zòng)、<u>划龙舟</u>(zhōu)。很多地方都举行龙舟<u>比赛</u>(jǔ hold)(sài)，非常(fēi cháng very)热闹(rè nao lively)。

Vocabulary:

1. 粽子 a pyramid shaped dumpling made with sticky rice wrapped in reed leaves

2. 划龙舟 dragon boat racing

3. 比赛 contest, tournament

165

Answer these questions about 端午节.

1. 端午节是农历的几月几号？

   _____。

2. 端午节人们吃什么？

   _____。

3. 端午节人们做什么？

   _____。

Math Problem!

端午节，有五个队比赛划龙舟，每个队有六个人。一共有多少个人划龙舟？

gòng
altogether

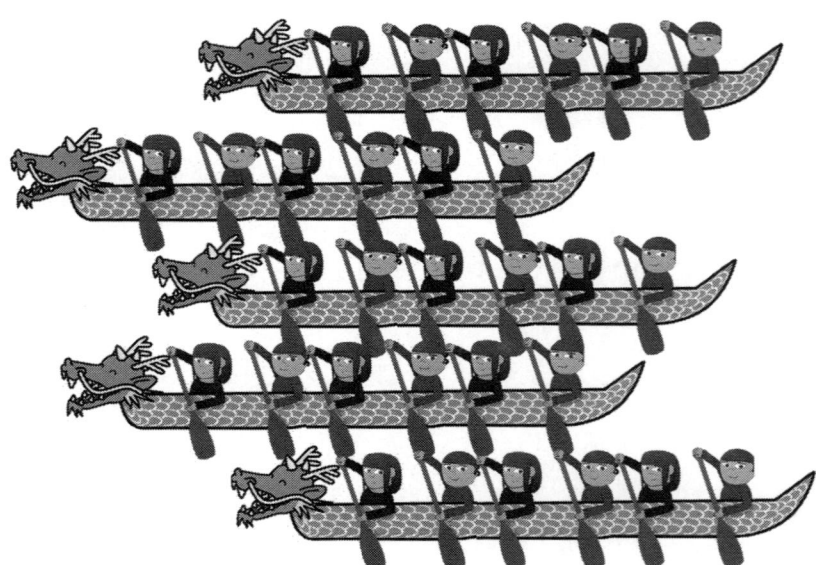

____ x ____ = ____

答：_____。

| Mid-Autumn Festival 中秋节 | 人文 People and Culture |

Read about 中秋节 and answer the questions.

中秋节是农历的八月十五。中秋的意思就是秋天过了一半。十五的月亮又大又圆，非常(fēi cháng)漂亮。中秋节的晚上，大家吃月饼，看月亮，讲(jiǎng tell)关于(guān yú about)月亮的故事。

Vocabulary:

月饼　moon cake

1. 中秋节是农历的哪一天？

   _____。

2. "中秋"是什么意思？

   _____。

3. 中秋节人们吃什么？做什么？

   _____。

167

Quiz Time!

What holiday is it? Read the description and write down the name of each holiday in the parenthesis.

除夕　　新年　　元宵节　　端午节　　中秋节

1. 吃粽子，划龙舟。　（　　　　　）

2. 吃月饼，看月亮。　（　　　　　）

3. 吃元宵，猜灯谜。　（　　　　　）

4. 全家一起吃年夜饭。（　　　　　）

5. 穿新衣，去拜年。　（　　　　　）

Look at the pictures and write down the 12 animals for the Chinese zodiac.

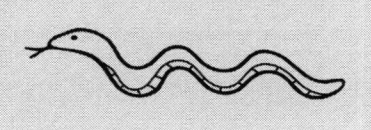

_____   _____   _____

_____   _____   _____

_____   _____   _____

_____   _____   _____

Congratulations!

祝贺_____小朋友！

你完成了《小手写中文》二年级的学习。

特发此证，以资鼓励。

Prerequisite Test for Level 3

Are you ready for the next level?

Read each character aloud and tell its meaning in English, or say it in a word/sentence in Chinese. As you go along, color in the boxes for the characters you know.

骑	驮	金	钉	刀	划	球	琴	竹	笔
弓	弹	弯	热	黑	禾	种	科	红	绿
盘	盖	肉	脸	背	您	忘	怕	怪	行
往	这	收	放	国	圆	院	那	邻	问
闪	广	床	库	病	疼	痒	礼	票	东
西	南	北	远	近	快	慢	新	旧	对
错	真	假	胖	瘦	轻	重	空	满	浅
深	浮	沉	粗	细	宽	窄	很	更	最
太	先	再	着	过	又	只	还	能	给
洋	洲	万	亿	鼠	虎	兔	龙	猴	猪
说话	时候	或者	可以	语言	农历	除夕	新年	元宵	端午

If you've colored 100 or more boxes, congratulations! You may now move on to the next level! If not, don't feel discouraged. Take some time to review this book. Once you are comfortable with the material, take this test again and sure enough, you'll move on!

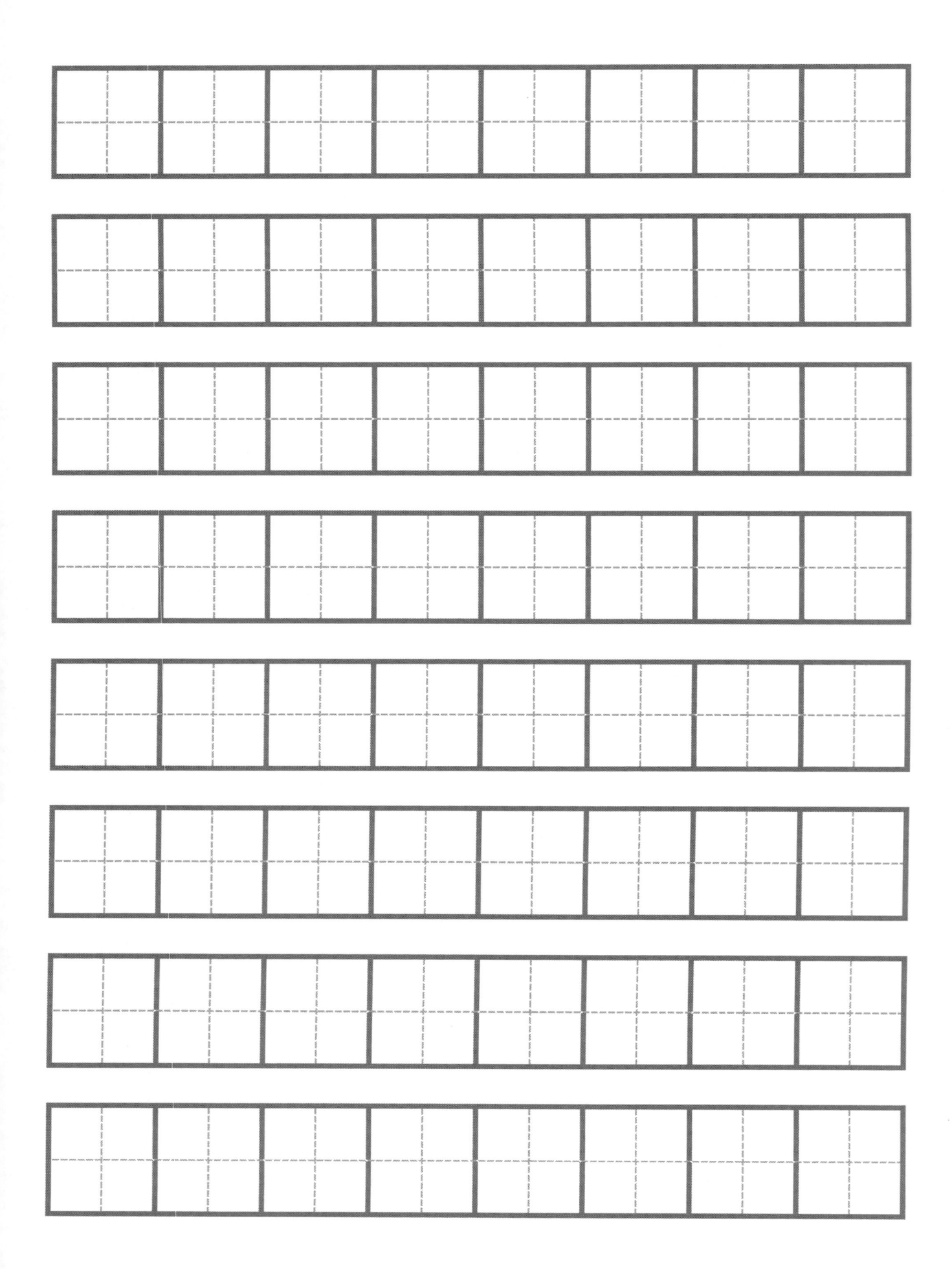

Made in the USA
Middletown, DE
02 July 2021